MAHÂBODHI
OR
THE GREAT BUDDHIST TEMPLE
UNDER
THE BODHI TREE
AT
BUDDHA-GAYA

MAHÂBODHI
OR
THE GREAT BUDDHIST TEMPLE
UNDER
THE BODHI TREE
AT
BUDDHA-GAYA

MAJOR GENERAL SIR A. CUNNINGHAM

GYAN

Published by

Gyan Publishing House
5, Ansari Road
Daryaganj, New Delhi-110002
Phone: 011-47034999, 9811692060
E-mail: books@gyanbooks.com

Distribution Network
gyanbooks.com
India, USA, Canada, UK, Australia

ISBN: 978-93-7097-051-9 (PB)
First Published, 1892

2nd Impression 2025

Printed at: Gyan Press, Delhi.

MAHÂBODHI OR THE GREAT BUDDHIST TEMPLE UNDER THE BODHI TREE AT BUDDHA-GAYA

Author: MAJOR GENERAL SIR A. CUNNINGHAM

MAHÂBODHI

OR

THE GREAT BUDDHIST TEMPLE

UNDER

THE BODHI TREE

AT

BUDDHA-GAYA

BY

MAJOR-GENERAL SIR A. CUNNINGHAM, R.E., K.C.I.E., C.S.I.

The Buddhists look upon the Bo Tree as most Christians look upon the Cross.
RHYS DAVIDS.—*Life of Gautama.*

The Bodhi Tree, thenceforward in all years
Never to fade, and ever to be kept
In homage of the world, beneath whose leaves
It was ordained that truth should come to Buddh.
EDWIN ARNOLD.—*Light of Asia.*

Slowly the Prince advanced,—beneath his tread,
At every step th' expectant world shook,
Until he rested 'neath the Bodhi Tree—
At once the trembling universe was still
Acknowledging the thronement of its lord.
A. C.

LONDON:
W. H. ALLEN & Co., LIMITED, 13, WATERLOO PLACE, S.W.
Publishers to the India Office.

1892.

CONTENTS.

PLATES.

PREFACE.

In 1878, when Dr. Râjendra Lâla Mitra published his work on the Temple of Buddha Gayâ, the only excavations which had then been made were the trenches dug by Major Meade in 1863 at my suggestion, and the subsequent surface clearances by the Burmese. The former had exposed the foundation lines of the original Buddhist Railing, which once surrounded the Temple, while the latter had brought to light several small Temples, besides many votive Stûpas and Buddhist Statues.

I visited Buddha Gayâ in 1879 for the express purpose of seeing what had been done by the Burmese. Their clearances had not been carried deep enough to expose the more ancient monuments which still existed on or near the original level of the ground on which the Temple was built. The clearances also had not been made with any discrimination. Everything was removed as it became exposed; and thus many of the hemispherical domes of the rows of early votive Stûpas were thrown down. Fortunately they were not carried away, and when the great clearance of the ruins was subsequently made by Mr. Beglar, many of these stone hemispheres were restored to their original Stûpas, the remains of which had not been disturbed.

The ruinous state of the Temple at this time was thus described by a correspondent of the "Calcutta Englishman" newspaper:—"I found the Temple in the following "condition: The whole of the plinth and lower mouldings buried under accumulations "of rubbish; the floor of the sanctum, and of the great hall in front 4 feet lower "than the level of a rough stone floor laid by the Burmese, who had partially cleared "away the heaps of rubbish in front, the great hall roofless; the half-hall, or porch of "the second storey, roofless; the whole of the front of the Temple above the level of "the third chamber fallen, disclosing a great triangular gap, about 20 feet high and

" 12 feet wide at base; the stairs leading up from lowest floor, or ground floor or
" terrace, from which the tower springs, roofless; the whole of the façade of the
" platform to the East a mound of ruins; the whole south façade of platform ruinous,
" but retaining here and there portions of original work; the entire West face of the
" platform of the Temple buried under rubbish, which itself was held up by a
" revetment wall 32 feet high of plain brick and mortar, unplastered, and looking for
" all the world like a dilapidated jail wall. The holy tree at the apex of a series of
" a circle of steps, which stood on the rubbish so held up by the revetment aforesaid,
" and the entire north wall above the then ground level a plain blank wall of mud and
" and brickbats, which was even then leaning outwards. A massive new well-plastered
" staircase [is] stuck on the East front or main façade at its north-east angle to
" give access to the terrace of the upper chamber, and to the holy tree. . . . .
" The entire West face of main tower peeled off, including the half of the upper
" pinnacle, the rest of pinnacle overhanging. The entire North face of tower, except
" the upper portion, peeled off; the East face in fair order above the great triangular
" gap already noticed; the South face in fairish order, the terrace or platform
" extensively cracked in all directions, the corbelled work in the third chamber,
" interior, overhanging in a most dangerous condition, the chamber at the same time
" being inaccessible."

Such was the state of the Great Buddhist Temple in 1880, when Sir Ashley Eden, the Lieut.-Governor of Bengal, appointed Mr. J. D. Beglar to make a thorough repair of the whole building. The work was begun during the course of the year with a further clearance of the accumulated rubbish, which had become absolutely necessary, as every year the interior of the Temple was turned into a small tank by the catchment of rain water from the outside. During this clearance the different additions made to the outside were revealed. At the same time the interior pavement, which had become very uneven, was taken up to be relaid; and this work brought to light the numerous alterations which had been made at different times to the inside of the Temple.

In February 1881 I paid another visit to the Temple, and I was present when the discovery of Relics was made under the front of the Vajrâsan Throne. As the discoveries that were made during these excavations are described in detail in the following pages, I will here only state the principal conclusions which I was constrained to adopt on their evidence.

B.C. 250.—The first, and perhaps the most interesting, discovery was the remains of the original Temple of Asoka, with the polished Vajrâsan Throne, exactly as portrayed in the Bharhut Basrelief with the view of the Bodhi Tree of Sâkya-muni.

Close by, on the north side of the Temple, was found the remains of the cloistered walk, with its 22 pillared bases still in situ, each marked with a letter of the Indian alphabet of Asoka from *a* to the cerebral *t*. One shaft was also found marked with the Asoka letter *a*.

But the most important discovery was the fact that the present Temple is built exactly over the remains of Asoka's Temple, so that the original Vajrâsan Throne still retains its old position of Buddha's seat, and the reputed centre of the Universe.

A.D. 140.—The age of the present Great Temple is shown by the presence of a gold coin of the Indo-Scythian King Huvishka, amongst the Relics deposited in front of the Throne, along with some silver punch-marked coins. The date of Huvishka is now known as covering a large portion of the first half of the 2nd century A.D. The same age is declared by the presence of an Indo-Scythian inscription on the outer Vajrâsan Throne, and also by the discovery of a colossal statue, just outside the Temple, with an Indo-Scythian inscription dated in the year 64, which if referred to the Saka Samvat gives A.D. 78+64=142. I formerly thought that there was no Mahâbodhi Temple standing at the time of Fa-Hian's visit, A.D. 399 to 409; but I now see that his actual words distinctly imply that Temples were then standing at *all the four famous sites* connected with Buddha's history. These were—1. Birthplace at Kapila. 2. *The Bodhi Tree at Uruvilwa.* 3. The Deer-park at Benares. 4. Place of Death at Kusinagara. Fa Hian must therefore have seen the present Temple about one century and a half after its erection.

450 A.D. circa.—The early date of the Temple is proved by its straight sides, which form a *square* truncated pyramid, whereas all mediæval Temples that I have seen have curved or slightly bulging sides, which give a more graceful form. The entrance Pavilion in front of the Temple, which was seen by Hwen Thsang, and which he describes as an after addition, may perhaps be the work of King Sado, called *Thado-Meng* in the Burmese inscription. Some repairs must certainly have been made about this time, as we know that the pillared roof of Buddha's Walk had fallen down before the time of Hwen Thsang, who does not notice it.

About this time also must have occurred the great irruption of sand from the Phalgu River, which filled the whole courtyard of the Temple to a height of 2½ feet. To the same period I would refer the sandstone pavement of the interior, which I suppose was a necessary repair owing to the breaking up of the old terraced flooring of Huvishka's Temple. A great irruption of sand is alluded to by Hwen Thsang, who says, "Since the true Law has become weakened *sand and earth* have covered "the Adamantine Throne all over, and it is no longer visible;" to which he adds that "during the last century or two men will go towards the Bodhi Tree, as they can no "longer see the Adamant Throne." By this account I understand that at the time of the Pilgrim's visit the *Vajrâsan* Throne outside the Temple under the Bodhi Tree was covered with sand, and consequently men could not pay their devotion to it.[1]

A.D. 600.—In the beginning of the 7th century the Bodhi Tree was cut down by Raja Ṣaṣângka, the great opponent of Buddhism. At the same time the statue of Buddha inside must have been broken, although the pilgrim piously records that it was saved by a stratagem of Pûrna Varma's Minister.

A.D. 620.—The Bodhi Tree was afterwards restored by Raja Pûrna Varma, who surrounded it with a stone wall, about 24 feet high, to prevent it being again cut down. By this account I understand that the Raja placed his new Tree on the top of the basement terrace, about 25 feet above the level of the accumulated sand which surrounded the Temple. At the same time I conclude that he must have found the old Vajrâsan Stone, which had originally been placed on the broad terraced berm which surrounded the whole building. This Throne would then have been raised on the basement, 3½ feet in height, where it was found in 1881, hidden behind the mass of the great central buttress.

A.D. 1035 to 1079.—The next ascertained event in the history of the Temple is the account of the extensive repairs which were made by the Burmese in the 11th century. The detailed notice of this work is recorded by the Burmese themselves in an inscription dated in A.D. 1079. The earlier date of A.D. 1035 is found on a gilded copper umbrella top, which was the gift of Dharma Raja Guru, the person deputed by the King of Burma to repair the Temple. By the second inscription on a stone slab we learn that as the repairs were not finished by this officer, a second agent was sent in A.D. 1071, who succeeded in making a complete restoration in 7 years and 10 months, having finished the work in A.D. 1079.

Other repairs were no doubt made in the latter half of the 12th century by Asoka-balla, Raja of *Sapâda-laksha,* or Sawâlak, just before the Muhammadan conquest in A.D. 1198.

After this time I find no notices of Mahâbodhi. In the chronicles of Mewar mention is made of expeditions in the 13th and 14th centuries for the recovery of Gayâ

[1] Julien's Hwen Thsang, II., 401. Beal's Hwen Thsang, II., 116.

from the infidels; but these notices refer to Brahma Gayâ of the Brahmanists, and not to the Great Buddhist Temple of Buddha Gayâ. I, however, look upon these expeditions as pious wishes of the Bardic chroniclers.

In the six centuries which followed the Muhammadan conquest during which the Mahâbodhi Temple was quite deserted, it gradually became more and more ruinous. The greater part of the stucco facing had disappeared, and the brick walls, being laid only with clay mortar, had peeled off on all sides, more especially on the West face, where in many places the bricks had fallen away to a depth of nearly 5 feet. But a sufficient number of tolerably well-preserved portions of the mouldings and niches on the other faces still remained to enable the restorer to complete the repair of the whole in the exact pattern of the original. This extensive renewal of the surface was absolutely necessary to ensure the future safety of the building. No new features were added, the restoration being limited to a strict repetition of the existing niches and mouldings.

But the front Pavilion of the Temple was almost a complete ruin; and at first it did not seem likely that any authority could be found for even its partial renewal. My advice was that the ruined walls should be well plastered with cement simply to prevent further decay. This was actually begun, as I see by one of Mr. Beglar's photographs. But a short time afterwards a small model in stone of the Temple was found amongst the ruins, from which the whole design of the building as it existed in mediæval times could be traced with tolerable completeness [*See* Plate XVI.] From this model, and from the still existing remains of the façade, Mr. Beglar designed the front Pavilion as it now stands.[1] On the same authority he designed the four corner Pavilions, which are seen in all the photographs of the restored Temple. This additional work has been much criticised, and I have been roundly abused for it in company with Mr. Beglar, although I had nothing whatever to say to it. At the same time I must confess that, since I have seen it, I think his design of the front Pavilion is a very successful completion of the entrance in the style and spirit of the original work as shown in the model. It is of course a *Restoration*, which, as it was based on the double authority of existing remains and an ancient model, I consider as legitimate and justifiable.

---

[1] I have since discovered a second model of the Mahâbodhi Temple in the Indian Museum at Calcutta. As it was found at Mroboung, the ancient capital of Arakan, I have no doubt that models of the Temple were kept on sale for pilgrims.

The importance of the Mahâbodhi Temple for the history of Indian art is quite unique, as it gives us the oldest existing remains of both sculpture and architecture. The sculptures of the Bharhut Stûpa date from the flourishing period of the Sunga Dynasty, about B.C. 150, whereas the Mahâbodhi remains belong to the period of Asoka, just one century earlier.

There are two large statues, both alto-relievos, one of a female standing to the front on the corner pillar of Buddha's Walk, the other of a Yakshini in a tree, on a corner pillar of the Railing. Of smaller sculptures there are basso-relievos of the famous *Jetavano* garden scene, of the *Indra-sâla* cave, of the *Bodhi Tree,* and of the *Tri-ratna* and *Dharma-chakra* symbols. The remains of architecture are limited to the Pillars, which show unmistakeably their Persepolitan origin, both in their bulbous bases and in their animal capitals.

In Appendix A. I have added some notes on the peculiar construction of the Vaults and Arches of the Temple. As the style is confined to India, it may, very appropriately, be called the Indian Arch.

In Appendix B. I have suggested that the Plan of the Temple must have been formed on a diagram of squares after the usual Indian fashion.

MAHÂBODHI.

I.—HISTORICAL NOTICES.

The history of the Mahâbodhi Temple is written in the alterations and successive additions that were made to it. These different works are actual *facts* that were revealed during the repair of the building. The chief alteration was the removal of the upper slab of the Vajrâsan Throne from the inside to the outside of the Temple. As this slab is sculptured on all four faces it must have been exposed to view on all four sides in an open building. Another later change was the elevation of the Bodhi Tree from the ground level to the top of the basement, a rise of more than 24 feet. Other alterations were the successive changes in the level of the floors, both inside and outside, which were gradually raised from the time of Asoka down to the last great restoration of the Temple by the Burmese in the 11th century of the Christian era.

The most prominent additions were the three great buttresses built against the back wall of the basement. These subsisted in a ruined state down to the present time; but they had been completely detached from the Temple by their entire want of foundations, the lower courses being laid on the bare sand. Their weight failed to withstand the resistless force of the growing roots of the holy Pipal Tree, one of which that had penetrated in a slanting direction across one of the niche figures of Buddha was as thick as a man's thigh. The actual separation amounted to 6 or 8 inches, and the gap was filled with crushed bricks of the back wall. *See* Plate XV.

A much more striking addition must have been the front portico, which is described by Hwen Thsang as a pavilion of three storeys.[1] No remains of this work came down to our time save the edges of the crumbling walls that were attached to the main building. But the ground plan was plainly indicated by the bases of Pillars, which showed an open portico, similar to that which was added to the Great Temple at Nâlanda. The front of the portico consisted of four tall pillars, which, judging from the pilaster attached to the back wall must have been nearly plain. This front of four pillars is also clearly shown in the small model of the Temple which was found amongst the ruins.[2]

The site on which this famous Temple stood is said to have been pointed out by Upa Gupta to Asoka, who gave 100,000 pieces of gold for the building.[3] This site was

[1] Beal's Si-yu-ki, II. 218. [2] *See* Plate XVI. [3] Lalita Vistara.

near the small village of *Uruvilwa*, or *Uruwela* as it is called in the Pali Chronicles, and which still exists under the name of *Urel.* This place was then the residence of the eldest of the three Kâsyapa brothers, on which account he was known as Uruvilwa Kâsyapa. When the Prince Sâkya Sinha arrived there "he went to the residence of "Uruwela Kâsyapa," who was a fire-worshipper.[1] The name of Uruvilwa is not mentioned by the Chinese pilgrims; but it is found repeatedly in the Buddhist Chronicles of Ceylon; and in the Mahâwanso it is stated that Buddha-ghosha, on his return from Ceylon to India, went "to worship at the Bo Tree at Uruwelaya in "Magadha." There is some doubt about the meaning of Uruvilwâ, which Turnour translates as "sand hills" or "waves of land," from *uru* "sand," and *welaya* "waves "or mounds."[2] In the Tibetan version of the Lalita Vistara it is translated as "many tanks."[3] Both of these versions agree very well with the sandy nature of the site and its surrounding tanks. Uruvilwâ was the name of the village which was under a senâpati or senâni, named Nandika, whose daughter Sujâtâ presented the rice-and-milk to Buddha. In the Lalita Vistara nine other young girls are associated with Sujâtâ, of whom one is named *Uluvillikâ*. In some passages mention is made of the "forest of "Uruvilvâ," near which was a village of the same name. As *vilva* is the name of the common and well known tree now called "*bel*" (Aegle marmelos), the original meaning of Uruvilvâ would have been the "many *bel* trees," or the "*Bel* forest." This derivation is confirmed by the statement of the Lalita Vistara, according to which Buddha was charmed when he beheld the village of Uruvilvâ with its *beautiful trees and shrubs*, and the pure waters of the Nairanjana River. Unfortunately this stream is liable to sudden inundations during the rainy season. That it was equally subject to great floods in early times is, I think, proved by the story of Kâsyapa's anxiety for Buddha's safety when surrounded by the inundation. The deposit of sand about Uruvilvâ seems also to be established by the following legend:—

"In a former age there were ten thousand ascetics resident in that forest, and it "was their custom that when any of them were troubled with evil thoughts, they "arose early in the morning, and going to the river, entered it, and waded on until "the water reached to their mouths, when they took up a handful of sand from the "bottom and put it in a bag. They afterwards confessed the fault of which they "had been guilty in the midst of the assembled ascetics, and threw down the sand "in their presence as a token that the appointed penance had been performed. By this "means, in the course of years, a sandy plain was produced 16 miles in size."

This certainly is an ingenious way of accounting for the accumulation of sand; but I prefer the natural process of the river floods, and I am willing to accept the 16 miles as a fair estimate of the extent of the sandy tract.

I got the first notice of the name of Mahâbodhi in the end of the year 1877, as I was approaching Buddha Gayâ from the south.[4] For several days I had heard mention of a lofty Temple called Mahâbodhi, which I soon found was the common name for the Great Temple of Buddha Gayâ. Everywhere the people spoke of it by no other name. I then came to the conclusion that this must have been its name in ancient times. This

---

[1] Hardy.—Manual of Buddhism, p. 189. Beal.—Romantic History of Buddha, p. 292.

[2] Mahawanso; Index, p. 27.

[3] Foucaux.—Lalita Vistara, p. 238.

[4] *See* Archæological Survey, 1877–78, Vol. XI., p. 141., where I have mentioned the fact.

opinion was confirmed by a reference to Hwen Thsang's Travels, in which I found that the Temple was called the *Mo-ho-pu-ti*, or *Mahâbodhi Vihâra*, and the Monastery the *Mahâbodhi Sanghârâma*. I afterwards found that the same name was used by all the Chinese pilgrims of the 7th century,[1] of whose travels we have short notices by Mr. Beal.

The name of Mahâbodhi also occurs in a Brahmanical inscription found at Buddha Gayâ, which records a grant made in A.D. 850 by Raja Dharma Pâla.[2]

Still later it is found in two of the inscriptions of Raja Asokaballa, of which one is dated in A.D. 1157[3] according to my reckoning.

Lastly, the name of Mahâbodhi is found in *all* the inscriptions of the granite pavement slabs, which range in date from A.D. 1302 to 1331.

From these notices it appears that the name of Mahâbodhi was the common appellation for the holy site where Sâkya-Muni had attained Buddhahood. Of course the terms *Bodhi* and *Mahâbodhi* apply primarily to the holy Pipal Tree, or *Bodhi-drûma*.

Under these circumstances I have thought it right to drop the erroneous title of Buddha Gayâ, which is first found in the apocryphal inscription of Amara Deva.[4] Abul Fazl mentions Brahma Gayâ as a place of Hindu worship sacred to Brahmâ.[5] But the Great Temple of Mahâbodhi stands a short distance to the north of the village of *Urel* or *Uruvilwa*, 6 miles to the south of Gayâ, and has no connexion whatever with the name of Gayâ.

In giving the name of *Mahâbodhi* to the most famous place in Buddhist history, I am only restoring the true name which has been in use for many centuries. The simple form of Bodhi was in common use in the time of Asoka, and the holy Pipal Tree is so named in the Bharhut Basrelief, of B.C. 150, as the—

Bhagavato Saka-Munino Bodhi,

"the Bodhi (Tree) of the divine Sakya Muni." The larger name of *Mahâbodhi* has been in use for more than twelve centuries, from the time of the Chinese pilgrim, Hwen Thsang, in the 7th century down to the present day. The full name of the holy Pipal Tree was *Bodhi-drûma*, or the "Tree of Wisdom." The Throne or seat of Buddha, was called *Bodhi-maṇḍa;* the Temple erected over the Throne was named *Mahâbodhi Vihâra*, and the Great Monastery close by was called *Mahâbodhi Sanghârâma*. But perhaps the most decisive proof that *Mahâbodhi* was the true name of the place is the fact that it is so called in a Brahmanical inscription (Plate XXVIII., fig. 3) which records the setting up of an image of the four-faced Mahâdeva in A.D. 850, during the reign of Dharma Pâla "*for the benefit* of the inhabitants of *Mahâbodhi* [*Mahâbodhi-nivâsinâm*]."

---

[1] Indian Antiquary, Vol. X., pp. 109–192.
[2] *See* Plate XXVIII., No. 3.
[3] *See* Plate XXVIII., A.
[4] Asiatic Researches, I., 284.
[5] Gladwin's Ayin Akbari, III., 25.

II.—TEMPLE OF ASOKA.

All our authorities agree in referring the erection of the first Temple of Mahâbodhi to the great King, Asoka.[1] The old Burmese inscription, which records the successive repairs of the Temple, assigns the original building to Asoka. *See* Section XX., forward. Unfortunately we possess no description of it save a brief mention by the pilgrim Hwen Thsang, who says that it was "a small Vihâra," and that Asoka "surrounded "the Bodhi Tree with a stone wall about 10 feet in height," which was still standing in A.D. 637, when he visited Mahâbodhi. We learn further that the circuit of the Vajrâsan or holy area, in the middle of which stood the sacred Bodhi Tree, was about 100 paces, or 250 feet.

Fortunately amongst the Basreliefs of the ruined Stûpa at Bharhut there are two sculptured representations of Asoka's Temple with the holy Pipal Tree behind it, one of which is duly labelled as "*Bhagavato Sâka Munino Bodhi*," or "Bodhi Tree of the blessed Sâkya Muni."[2] As the sculptures of the Bharhut Stûpa are certainly as old as B.C. 120 or 100, the Basreliefs must be tolerably faithful representations of the Temple, as accurate indeed as the skill of the artist was able to make them.

According to the inscribed Bharhut Basrelief this Temple of Asoka was an open pavilion supported on pillars. In the middle is seen the Vajrâsan Throne, decorated in front with four flat pilasters. Behind the Throne appears the trunk of the Bodhi Tree, which rises up high above the building, and on each side of the Tree there is a combined symbol of the *Tri-Ratna* and the *Dharma-Chakra*, standing on the top of a short pillar. On each side of the Vajrâsan room there is a side room of the same style. The top of the Throne is ornamented with flowers, but there is no figure of Buddha. *See* Plate III.

That the Bharhut Basrelief was a very fair representation of the actual Temple, was most clearly and satisfactorily proved during the repairs of the floor of the present Temple. As the granite pavement inside was very uneven it was absolutely necessary

---

[1] The old Burmese inscription which records the successive repairs of the Temple also refers the building of the original Temple to Asoka.

[2] Stûpa of Bharhut, Pl. XXXI., fig. 3. Mr. Thomas, in one of his cranky moods (Early Faith of Asoka, p. 8.—Note) has objected to the date which I have assigned to the Bharhut sculptures in the following terms :—"It is *scarcely necessary* for me to add that I by no means concur in the early date attributed by General "Cunningham to these sculptures." To rebut this sneering remark I need only refer to the fact that the Toran Gateways of the Bharhut Stûpa were erected by Danabhuti, King of the *Sungas*, whose dynasty succeeded the Mauryas, and ruled over N. India from B.C. 178 to 66, within which period lies the date which I have assigned to the Stûpa.

that it should be taken up and relaid. The blue stone-facing of the Throne, which stood on this pavement, was therefore carefully removed, and the whole of the granite pavement taken up. When this was done it was found that there was a second Throne behind, with a plaster facing much broken and shattered. Behind this again there was a third Throne of *polished* sandstone, with four short pilasters in front, exactly as depicted in the Bharhut Basrelief.

On removing the whole of the plaster from the sandstone front a very startling discovery was made, which proved unmistakably that the sandstone Throne must be older than the present Temple. This discovery was the fact that the sandstone Throne did not stand on the centre line of the present Temple, its south end being only 20 inches from the south wall of the Chamber while its northern end was as much as 39 inches from the northern wall; the difference being 1 foot 7 inches. *See* Plate VI.

Another startling discovery was also made in the fact that the plaster-faced Throne was lengthened at the northern end by 19 inches, so as to place it exactly in the middle of the present Chamber. Here, then, was a clear and convincing proof that the sandstone Throne must be of older date than the present Temple.

This conclusion was soon afterwards made still more positive by the discovery in situ of two Persepolitan pillar bases, one on each side of the sandstone Throne at equal distance from *its* ends, the southern base being partly under the south wall of the Chamber while the northern one was quite clear of the northern wall. These two bases were 10 feet 9½ inches apart from centre to centre. As the pillars were about 1 foot in diameter, the length of the architrave which covered them could not have been less than 12 feet.

Near the north-east corner of the present Chamber a third Persepolitan base was discovered, but not actually in situ, as it had been placed upside down so as to present its broad flat bottom as a part of the pavement.

Putting all these discoveries together, and comparing them with the view of Asoka's Temple, preserved in the Bharhut Basrelief, I cannot help feeling the conviction that we have found some of the actual remains of the original building.

The front view of the Throne is especially striking, and when we see that this was flanked by two Pillars of Asoka's age, the resemblance between the existing remains and the sculptured representation seems too close to be accidental.

But further discoveries which were made tend to point very plainly to the same conclusion. These were the remains of old walls which were found under the basement of the present Temple on the west, the south, and the east sides, the last being the most interesting and conclusive.[1] Here we found not only the remains of the old walls, but also the peculiar semicircular Step, which is a marked feature of all the doorways and gateways of the early buildings. Here, then, we have the entrance of Asoka's Temple, and, as it lies within the remains of the old wall, I conclude that these remains of old walls mark the lines of plinth of the Railing which surrounded Asoka's Temple. On the north side the line of Railing must necessarily have been inside the Cloistered Walk, which still exists. We thus obtain the dimensions of the enclosure which surrounded the Vajrâsan. Its central line is determined by drawing a line from the middle of the

[1] *See* Plate II., where these old remains of walls are marked F^1, F^2, F^3. The Step is marked S.

polished sandstone Vajrâsan through the middle of the semicircular Step which formed the entrance to the Temple. Taking this line as the central line of the Vajrâsan area, the northern line of Railing will fall just to the south of the Cloistered Walk. As this central line is parallel to the line of the Cloistered Walk itself, which is undoubtedly of the age of Asoka, we see that the walls of the new Temple deviated slightly from the old lines of Asoka's Vihâra.

A collateral proof of the correctness of the area thus assigned to Asoka's Railing is found in the dimensions given by Hwen Thsang to the circuit of the true Vajrâsan area, which he says was about 100 paces or 250 feet. The actual circuit of the enclosure derived from the remains of the three old walls is 258 feet measured outside [73 feet long by 56 broad], or 248 feet measured inside [68 feet long 56 broad].

The Pillars in the Plan have been arranged on these old walls at the same distances as in the Railing of the present Temple, as all the old Pillars and Rail Bars and Copings of Asoka's Railing were made use of as far as they would go. The result is that, after leaving an opening on the east side for the entrance, the Pillars thus arranged number 64. As this was a very favourite number with the Hindus, it affords another strong proof for the correctness of the proposed arrangement.

Another collateral proof is the fact that the centre of the old Vajrâsan Throne is exactly in the centre of this old enclosure, which agrees with the statement of Hwen Thsang.[1] "In the *middle* of the enclosure surrounding the Bodhi Tree is the Diamond "Throne [Vajrâsana]." Julien says that it was *exactly in the middle* "juste au milieu "des murs qui entourent l'arbre de l'intelligence [Bodhidrûma]."[2] It was also believed to be in the very centre of the 3,000 grand chiliocosms.

Taking all these agreements of arrangements and dimensions with the ascertained age of the old Throne and its Pillars, I think there can be no reasonable doubt that we have now discovered the actual remains of the original Temple of Asoka.

After comparing these existing remains with the Bharhut Basrelief I have ventured to sketch an outline plan of what I suppose the Asoka Temple may have been.[3]

The size of the middle room in which stood the Vajrâsan Throne, V, is determined by the positions of the two Pillar bases P^1 and P^2, which are 9 feet $10\frac{1}{2}$ inches from centre to centre. As the architrave which covered them could not have been less than 12 feet in length, I conclude that this centre room must have been 12 feet broad, and twice as long, because the pillar on each side of the Vajrâsan Throne stood opposite the middle of its side, as shown in Plate II. The size of the four side rooms is, I think, pretty clearly shown by the position of the Pillar base, P^3, as well as by the semicircular Step, S, which could only have been at the entrance. These data give 9 feet for the breadth, thus making the whole size of the Temple just 42 feet by 30 feet, the roof being supported on 12 pillars. In plan it would have been a Greek cross.

The position of the Bodhi Tree must have been inside at B, immediately behind the Vajrâsan Throne, as in several sculptures the Bodhi Tree is apparently represented as coming through the roof of the Temple. This is well shown in a second Bharhut Basrelief,[4] which I take to be a back view of the actual Bodhi Tree of Sâkya Muni at

[1] Beal's Si-yu-ki, II., 115, 116. [2] Julien's Hwen Thsang, II., 460.
[3] *See* Plate II., and compare with the Bharhut Basrelief in Plate III.
[4] Stûpa of Bharhut, XXXI., fig. 3, and fig. 2, Plate III. of this volume.

Mahâbodhi. My reasons for thinking so are the triple doorway and the Elephant Pillar on the right hand. It is true that no trace of any Elephant Pillar has been found; but as its position, according to both of the basreliefs, was close to the north-east corner of the present Temple, somewhere about M in the plan, its remains must now be under the walls of the present Temple, as shown by the letters B B B B at each of its outer corners.

The remains of Asoka's surrounding wall were found at F^1, F^2, and F^3. These remains were discovered by making small openings in the outer faces of the plinth or basement of the present Temple. I was induced to make them in the hope of finding some traces of the old Temple. They were, of course, made at my own expense, and I am glad to say that they were eminently successful, as they brought to light, on two sides, some portions of the plinth of Asoka's surrounding Railing. At F^1 on the west, at a distance of 3½ feet inside the mass of the basement, the old wall, 2½ thick, was traced for a length of 9 feet. On the south side at F^2, near the south-west corner, the old wall was found at distance of only 1 foot 2 inches inside the mass of the present basement. A third portion was discovered on the east side at F^3 on taking up the pavement of the passage leading into the present Temple. The limits of the surrounding wall were thus satisfactorily determined on the west, south, and east sides, while the northern side was laid down by a line equidistant with the south wall from the centre of the Vajrâsan Throne. As this line falls within the Cloistered Walk [which will be described presently], the size of the original area surrounding the Vajrâsan has, I think, been very satisfactorily determined.

In taking up the pavement of the passage, as I have already stated, the semicircular Step, marked S, was also discovered, and by drawing a line from the centre of this Step to the centre of the Vajrâsan Throne, the eccentricity of the line of the east and west alignment of the remains of Asoka's Railing was found to be the same as that of Buddha's Cloistered Walk outside with respect to the walls of the present Temple. This agreement shows that the foundations of the old enclosure must be of the same age as the Cloistered Walk, and must therefore be a part of the work made in the time of Asoka. A very striking confirmation of the accuracy of the ground plan of Asoka's Temple, as thus obtained, is shown by drawing two diagonal lines across the enclosure. As these two lines cross exactly on the middle of the polished sandstone Throne we see the accuracy of the pilgrim's description that the Diamond Throne was placed in the middle of the *Bodhi-manda*, a Holy Enclosure which surrounded the Bodhi Tree. *See* Plate II.

III.—BUDDHA'S WALK.

The raised terrace, on which Buddha took exercise, was one of the commonest monuments at every Buddhist site where Buddha had once lived. The most famous of these promenades was that near the Bodhi Tree of Uruvilwa, where Buddha walked for seven days from east to west. This famous pathway was called "*Chankramana Chaitya*," or in Pâli, *Chankamo*.[1] This term means simply the place of the "slow or meditative walk," but is generally accepted as "the Covered or Cloistered Walk," and in later times it was called the "Jewelled Cloister."

All the authorities agree as to the position of the walk. After Sâkya had attained Buddhahood he did not rise from his seat, but remained for seven days in meditation. He then rose, says Hwen Thsang, and going to the *North* of the Tree, he walked up and down from east to west for exercise, for about 10 paces, or 25 feet.[2] Here the pilgrim has clearly made a mistake, as he afterwards states that 18 wonderful flowers sprang up under his footprints. According to this latter statement Buddha must have taken not less than 17 paces. I would, therefore, correct the first statement to 20 paces or 50 feet, which would agree with the actual length, 53 feet, of the terraced walk that still exists. According to the pilgrim the Walk was a brick wall about 3 feet high, which is an exact description of it at the present day. *See* Plates II. and V.

The Walk was in existence in the time of Fa Hian, who mentions the monument where Buddha walked backwards and forwards for seven days under the *Pei-to-tree*.[3]

This cloistered walk which still exists close to the north side of the Temple is a simple brick wall, 53 feet long, 3 feet 6 inches broad, and a little more than 3 feet in height. On each side there is a row of 11 Persepolitan Pillar-bases, of the well-known pattern of a vase placed above three or four steps, and surmounted by a parabolic moulding with an octagonal top for the reception of an octagonal shaft. Each of these bases was marked with a separate letter of the Asoka alphabet, the 11 bases on the south side bearing the 11 vowels, *a, â, i, î, u, û, e, ai, o, au, ah,* and the northern bases, the first 11 consonants *k, kh, g, gh, ng, ch, chh, j, jh, ny, t*. In Plate V. I have given one of the Bharhut Basreliefs, which I feel certain must be a representation of one of these covered walks. In the same Plate I have given a view of the remains of Buddha's Walk at Mahâbodhi. The whole length of the Walk

---

1 Mahawanso, pp. 38–161.

2 Julien's Hwen Thsang, II., 470.

3 Giles's Fa Hian, p. 76. It was also known as the "Jewelled Cloister." *See* Rhys Davids' Jâtaka, quoting the Nidâna-kathâ, p. 106. "Then he created, between the Throne and the spot where he had stood, a *Cloistered* " *Walk*, and he spent seven days walking up and down in that '*Jewelled Cloister*,' which stretched from east " to west. And that spot became known as the Dâgoba of the *Jewelled Cloister*."

is given with the northern row of Pillar bases still in situ, and the broken shaft placed on the end base. The Walk itself was still visible in Hwen Thsang's time (A.D. 640); but the pillar bases were then covered by a plastered terrace. This arrangement of letters has an important bearing on the antiquity of the Indian alphabet, as it shows that the several characters had already been arranged in their present groups as gutturals, palatals, cerebrals, dentals, labials, semi-vowels, and sibilants. The southern row of these bases was partly hidden under the basement of the Great Temple which had been built over them, on a slightly different alignment, part of the two most westerly bases alone appearing 7 inches outside the wall, while all the easterly bases were completely covered.

As these Pillar-bases showed that the Walk had once been roofed over, I made diligent search for some remains of the Pillars, and I was fortunate enough to light upon an octagonal shaft with a female figure on it, which had been brought to light by Mr. Beglar's excavations. On measuring the bottom of the shaft I was delighted to find that it was of the same dimensions as the recessed tops of the bases. The westerly base of the southern row, which bore the Asoka letter A, was therefore extracted, and when the octagonal shaft was set upon it, it was found to fit so exactly that there could be no doubt that the two pieces belonged to the same Pillar. This proved to be the case when, turning the shaft round for a better view, it was found to be marked with the same letter A as the base on which it was then standing. No fragments of other shafts have yet been found; but on looking about for other pieces that might have belonged to the capitals, several fragments were discovered which almost certainly belonged to these Pillars. All these fragments have been put together in their presumed places in Plate IV. The portion of the Bell capital and the remains of the squatted Lions seem to me to be quite certain. In the same plate I have given two basreliefs from the square pillars of the Railing for the illustration of the Pillars used in the Asoka architecture. All the members correspond exactly. The bases have the same globular tops, standing on a series of small steps. The shafts are octagonal, and the capitals have the usual bell-shaped tops, supporting a pair of recumbent animals placed side by side, with their faces outwards. Above their backs springs a conventional flowered ornament, which supports an oblong abacus. A good specimen of this style may be seen in the Gateway Pillars of the Bharhut Stûpa.[1] I think it probable that only the four corner pillars had sculptures upon them, and that all the others, being simple octagonal shafts, were carried off after the fall of the canopy, and used for other buildings. There is a notable instance of this kind of appropriation in a Temple doorway of the Gupta period from the Mahâbodhi ruins, one jamb of which was originally a pillar of the Asoka Railing, as proved by the segmental holes in its side for the reception of the Rail bars. This doorway is now in the Indian Museum, Calcutta, with a short Gupta inscription opening with the usual formula, "*deya dharmmâyam.*"

In Plate V., fig. 1, I have given a view of one of these Canopied Walks of Buddha from a Bharhut Basrelief. At first I thought that this sculpture was a representation of the Thrones of the Four Buddhas; but I now see that it gives a very good picture

---

[1] The Stûpa of Bharhut, Plates X., XI., and XII.

of a "Cloistered Walk." The flowers carved on the top are intended to mark the spots of Buddha's footprints. They are placed in two rows, apparently to show the right and left footsteps. The Mahâbodhi Walk was also called the "Jewelled Cloister," most probably on account of the strings of jewels with which pious pilgrims decorated it. Perhaps the pendant garlands shown in the basrelief may represent some of these strings of jewels.

As Hwen Thsang does not mention the canopied roof of Buddha's Walk, I conclude that it could not have had one in his time. But that the Walk certainly had a canopied roof at first is shown by the two rows of Pillar-bases, one on each side, which are still in situ, marked with letters of the Asoka alphabet.

I conclude that the roof must have been of wood, as a stone roof would have been difficult to construct, as well as very heavy and costly. In Plate V. I have given a view of one of these Promenade terraces from a Bharhut Basrelief. I make out from this representation that the ends must have been gabled. But there is nothing save the small ends of the longitudinal beams to show absolutely whether the roof was of stone or of wood. From the small ends of these longitudinal beams, as seen in the gables, I gather that the roof must almost certainly have been of wood. In Plate IV. I have given sketches of two stones, marked A and B, which were found in the pavement inside the Temple. They must certainly have belonged to the Asoka Temple, as the ornament of long beads on A is peculiar to his time.

IV.—ASOKA TEMPLE RAILING.

The only other remains of Asoka's time consist of the Pillars, Rail Bars, and Copings of the Colonnade or Railing which once enclosed the Vajrâsan Temple. According to Hwen Thsang, Asoka surrounded the holy Pipal Tree with a *stone* wall 10 feet high. Mr. Beal[1] also translates *stone*, but adds within brackets the word *brick*, without giving any reason for the correction. The actual remains of the stone Railing still exist, the only *brick* portion, as I have already pointed out, being the plinth on which the stone Railing stood. These brick remains, which are marked F[1], F[2], and F[3] in Plate II., were all found under the solid basement of the present Temple. As I have already stated, they prove that the circuit of the Railing was as nearly as possible 250 feet, which agrees exactly with the number of 100 paces or 250 feet given by Hwen Thsang, if his measurement refers to the Temple of Asoka.

The Pillars of the present Railing are proved to have belonged to the original Railing by their inscriptions in Asoka characters, which are also found on the Rail Bars and Copings. The shafts average about 14 inches by 12 inches in section, the corner pillars being perfect squares of $14\frac{1}{4}$ inches each side. The average distance from centre to centre of the pillars was about 3 feet 11 inches, and as the existing pieces of plinth foundation show a circuit of from 253 to 255 feet, an arrangement of 64 Pillars would cover 63 spaces plus two half pillars, or just 246 feet 9 inches, leaving an opening of 6 feet to 8 feet for an entrance on the east side. The Gateway openings of the Great Temple are 8 feet 8 inches in clear width. This width corresponds very nearly with that of the Toran Gateway on the east side of the Temple, which is 8 feet 3 inches at the ground level, but as the Toran Pillars have a rapid slope, the clear width at 5 feet is exactly 8 feet 6 inches.

As this particular number of 64 is both a favourite and a fortunate one amongst the Hindus, its occurrence here seems to add another corroboration to the accuracy of the Plan of Asoka's Temple, which has been already determined from other sources.

Hwen Thsang describes the Railing which he saw as about 10 feet in height, which agrees with the dimensions of the present Railing, the Coping being 1 foot 2 inches, the Pillars 6 feet 8 inches, and plinth 2 feet 2 inches, or altogether 9 feet 10 inches in height. Of course, the Railing standing in his time was that of the Great Temple, which still exists, although in a very incomplete state. But many of the Pillars, Rail Bars, and Copings are undoubtedly those of the Asoka Railing, which was re-arranged,

[1] Si-yu-ki, II., 118.

and its circuit very extensively enlarged to suit the greater dimensions of the surrounding enclosure of the new Temple, which is nearly 530 feet in circuit. That the inscribed portions of this Railing belonged to the original enclosure of Asoka is quite certain, as the Asoka inscriptions still remain on them distinct and legible. I described and figured several of the coping pieces some years ago.[1] A few pieces have since been discovered, of which two bear a new inscription of Asoka's time, as will be noticed presently.

The inner faces of the architraves or coping stones are ornamented with long strings of animals, some natural, but others quite fabulous. There are Elephants and Lions, Bulls and Deer, Goats and Sheep, mingled with Winged Horses and Fishtailed Elephants, Lions, and Rams. These are accompanied by some weather-worn inscriptions of Indo-Scythian or very early Gupta date, which no doubt belong to the period of the re-arrangement of the Railing after the building of the Great Temple. *See* Plate XXVII.

The outer faces of the coping are ornamented with continuous bands of flowers, and on two pieces there are rather long inscriptions of the Asoka period.

The Pillars are decorated after the usual fashion of early Buddhist Railings. On each face at top and bottom there are semicircular medallions, containing half flowers, or small scenes of various kinds. In the middle of each face there is a full circular medallion, which is ornamented in the same manner as the semicircular medallions. On the outer faces of several of these pillars there is a short inscription in Asoka characters, giving the name of the pious donor. The edges of all the middle pillars are bevelled. The corner pillars at the Gateways are perfectly square in section, with rectangular panels containing various scenes.

The Rail Bars are of the usual double curved section to fit into the almond-shaped holes in the side of the Pillars. They are ornamented on both faces with full circular bosses or medallions, containing flowers or Kings' busts, or animals, or capitals of Pillars. A few bear short inscriptions in Asoka characters.

On a single Pillar, which I dug up in 1871 near the south east corner of the Railing, there is a full length figure of a Yakshini clinging to a tree, with her right foot supported by a male figure. *See* Plate VII.

There is considerable variety in the subjects depicted in these small medallions. I have given two Plates of their basreliefs, which, though small, are of great interest as they are at least one hundred years older than the basreliefs of the Bharhut Stûpa. Amongst them I find illustrations of the famous *Kalpa-drûma*, or "wishing tree," of the legend of the *Indra-Sâla-guha*, and of the story of Anâthapindika's purchase of the *Jetavana* garden at Srâvasti.

In Plate VIII. I have given twelve specimens of the more interesting medallions which I will now try to describe.

No. 1.—A Bodhi Tree with umbrellas and garlands.

No. 2.—A combined symbol of the *Tri-ratna*, or "Three Gems," and the *Dharma Chakra* or "Wheel of Religion," set up on a throne and attended by two worshippers.

---

[1] Archæological Survey, Vol. III., Plate XXXVIII., and p. 99.

No. 3.—The *Dharma Chakra* symbol alone, supported on a Persepolitan Pillar capital of two animals back to back, with lotus flowers and garlands on each side.

No. 4.—The famous *Kalpa-drûma*, or "Wishing Tree." *Kalpa* was the name of a particular tree in *Swarga*, the paradise of Indra, which was supposed to grant all one's desires. I have already published a very curious sculptured capital of this tree, which gives quite a different representation of it.[1] This capital, which is now in the Indian Museum, stood, when I found it, on the bank of the Betwa River in Mâlwa, a short distance below Besnagar. The Tree is represented as a Banian with long pendent roots from which untold wealth, in the shape of square pieces of money, is dropping in such quantities that all the vessels placed below are full to overflowing. In the Mahâbodhi sculpture the subject is treated quite differently. Here two human arms are extended from the Tree, one holding a plate with food, and the other a pitcher of wine or water, towards a man, who is stretching out his right hand to receive them. Between the man and the Tree there is a *Morha*, or small wicker stool, with a small cross-legged table in front of it, for the use of the recipient. In the background there is a square block like an altar. The subject of the *Kalpa-drûma* is treated in the very same manner in the basrelief of the Bharhut Stûpa. *See* Plate VIII., fig. 11.

No. 5.—A Deva is represented flying over the battlements of a city, with a garland in his outstretched hand, towards a Bodhi Tree before which a man is kneeling in adoration.

No. 6.—This scene represents the famous *Indra-Sâla-guha*, where Indra's harper stands before the cave in which Buddha is living. This subject is also represented in one of the Bharhut Basreliefs,[2] to which I may refer for an explanation of the story of Indra's visit to Buddha in his "Hall Cave." The harper was named Panchasikha, or the "five crested." Buddha himself is not represented in either the Mahâbodhi or the Bharhut sculptures. His Seat is there, but it is empty.

No. 7.—This is a simple representation of the goddess Lakshmi standing to the front on a lotus, while she is being anointed by two Elephants. The same subject is treated in one of the Bharhut Basreliefs,[3] where however the goddess is represented sitting.[3] She is also represented on a large silver coin of the Indo-Scythian King Azilises, in my possession, standing in the same way as on this Mahâbodhi Basrelief. A duplicate of the standing goddess is found on one of the gateway Pillars of the south side. I find the same subject also on an old Hindu coin from Kosâmbi.

No. 8.—This is a very good portrayment of the well known scene in the Jetavana Garden at Srâvasti, of which there is a much larger representation amongst the Bharhut sculpture.[4] The scene shows the householder Anâthapindika and his servants engaged in covering the whole surface of the Jetavana, or Prince "Jeta's Garden," with golden *masurans*. The coins are all square pieces. The four trees are no doubt the sandal-wood trees which alone were left standing while all the other trees in the garden were cut down. On the right, one of the servants is carrying a basket full of coins to the two men who are spreading the square pieces over the ground. The story is given at length by Spence Hardy in his Manual of Buddhism, pp. 218–219, and in my Stûpa of Bharhut, with illustrative extracts by Professor Childers.

---

[1] Archæological Survey, vol. X., p. 43, and Plate XV.

[2] Stûpa of Bharhut, Plate XXVIII., fig. 4, and page 88.

[3] Stûpa of Bharhut, Plate XII.

[4] Stûpa of Bharhut, LVII., and p. 84.

No. 9.—A boat scene. The boat holds three men, of whom one is apparently engaged in poleing through a mass of lotus plants.

No. 10.—This is unfortunately broken. There are two females, of whom one is playing a Pandean pipe, while the other is holding up her right hand, as if marking time. There was a third figure in front, of whom only the head now remains, so that it is impossible even to guess at the subject with any probability.

No. 11.—This is a ploughing scene with a pair of bullocks, which might very well pass for a common field picture of the present day. In the courtyard of the Vishnu-pad Temple at Gayâ, there is another Buddhist Medallion with a similar scene. As its size corresponds with that of the Mahâbodhi Railing Medallions it must have been brought from thence.

No. 12.—A domestic scene. A King is seated in front with his right hand resting on his right knee, with the leg drawn up. His left hand is extended to receive some object which is being brought to him on a *banghi* pole carried by a bearer. Behind the king there is a female attendant with the usual *Chauri*.

In Plate IX. I have collected 23 specimens of minor subjects. Ten of them are lotus flowers of different patterns. Six Nos. 3, 4, 5, 7, 8, 11, are kings' heads. No. 10 is a grotesque face which fills the whole of the medallion. No. 12 is a curious figure with a human head and body, but with foliated legs and arms. No. 14 represents three Elephants bringing garlands to deposit at a Bodhi Tree. No. 15 is a winged Elephant. No. 17 shows a Lion in pursuit of a Deer. No. 18 presents a crocodile and No. 19 a winged Horse.

There are many other medallions with similar subjects, such as Stûpas, winged and other fabulous animals, and grotesque faces. The only one of any interest is a square panel on a mutilated corner pillar now in the arcade of the Mahant's residence. This offers a representation of the Sun in his four-horse chariot, attended by two females, who are shooting arrows to the right and left, which I take to symbolise the Sun's rays. A very good photograph of this scene is given in Plate 50 of Bâbu Râjendra Lâl's Buddha Gayâ.

Several other subjects are given in the illustrations which accompanied my First Report on Buddha Gayâ,[1] and a few others in Babu Rajendra Lal's work. Amongst them will be found Bodhi Trees, Stûpas, two Birds, and a Cow and Calf.

---

[1] Archæological Survey, Vol. I., Plates IX., X., and XI.

V.—INSCRIPTIONS ON ASOKA'S RAILING.

The most valuable parts of the Old Railing are its inscriptions, as their characters prove beyond all doubt that the Railing must be as old as the time of Asoka. And as we learn from Hwen Thsang that Asoka surrounded the Bodhi Tree with a stone enclosure, I conclude that the Railing which now exists must have formed part of his work. All these inscriptions are given in Plate X.

One of the short inscriptions is found repeated on several of the Pillars. I have given four examples of it in the accompanying Plate, Nos. 4, 5, 6, 7, all photographed from impressions. I read it as follows :—

Ayâye Kuraṅgiye dânam.

"Gift of the noble (lady) *Kuraṅgi.*"

I understand *Kuraṅgi* to be a female name, meaning "fawn-eyed," or with eyes like the Kuraṅgi Deer. One of the Jâtakas is named "*Kuraṅgi-Miga-Jâtaka*" after the Kuraṅgi Deer. We know also that the mother of Sâri-putra was named *Sârika,* because her eyes were like those of the Sâras (or Cyrus) bird. That this is the true explanation is proved by the two longer inscriptions, Nos. 8 and 9, which are found on pieces of the coping. I read the first part of these inscriptions as follows :—[1]

No. 8 . . . *Indâgi-Mitasa pajâvatiye Jivâputaye Kuraṅgiye dânam.*

No. 9 . . *ka putasa Indâgi-Mitasa pajâvatiye Jivâputaye Kuraṅgiye dânam,*

which I translate :

"Gift of Kuraṅgi, daughter of Jivâ, the sister-in-law of Indrâgni-Mitra, son "of ——— ka."

The first name is unfortunately imperfect; but the relationship of Kuraṅgi's mother, Jivâ to Indrâgni-Mitra, is unmistakeably declared by the word *pajâvati* (S. *prajâvati*), the "brother's wife." The first letter of the inscription would appear to have been *s*, thus making *saka putasa,* and it is quite possible that the name may have been Asoka, for in all the Eastern inscriptions of Asoka only one *s* is made use of.

[1] No. 8 is now in the Indian Museum at Calcutta. I have since learned that *Kuraṅgi* is still in use as a girl's name, "the fawn-eyed." My reading of *Kuraṅgi* as the name of a lady was made in November 1879, when I first saw the inscription No. 9. I am glad to find that the same reading has been made by Pandit Bhagwân Lâl. *See* Indian Antiquary, IX., 142, for 1880.

The latter part of this important record is missing. Following the word *dânam,* I read :—

Râja pâsâdâ Chetikâ sa . . "The royal Palace, the Chaitya," . The mention of the *Râja Pâsâdâ* would seem to connect the donor with the king's family. It would be besides only natural that members of the royal family should make gifts to the Temple which the king was building.

Babu Rajendra Lal has given a totally different rendering of this inscription. (*See* Catalogue of Indian Museum, Part I., p. 130.) He reads as follows :—

Gamitosa prajâvatiye jivaparaye Kuragiye dânam Ramopâsa dâna nikasâ.

which he translates :

"This gift, similar to that of Ramopâsa (is made by) Gamito to Kuragi, the lord "of living beings, and friend of creation."

There are two other short inscriptions on Rail Bars, which are of the usual form that has been made so familar by the similar records at Bharhut and Sânchi.

No. 2. *Amoghasa dânam.*

"Gift of Amogha."

No. 3. *Bodhi-rakhitasa Taba-panakasa dânam.*

"Gift of Bodhi-rakshita of Tambaparna (Ceylon)."

My reading of this inscription has been contested by Babu Rajendra Lâl, who says (Catalogue of Indian Museum, p. 127) :—"*The reading I copied from Cunningham is not* "*correct.* The first letter is *Bu*, not *Bo*, and the second *dha*, not *dhi*." This Rail Bar is now in the Indian Museum, and I have had the opportunity of examining the inscription again. My reading of *Bodhi* is undoubtedly correct, and so it has been pronounced by Pandit Bhagwân Lâl. *See* Indian Antiquary, Vol. IX., p. 142. But I assert with absolute certainty that my reading is correct, and that Rajendra Lâl's reading is wrong. I possess impressions of these inscriptions taken while the stone was still at Buddha Gayâ. And I have made fresh impressions in Calcutta.

At the top of the Plate, fig. 1, I have given facsimiles of the Asoka letters found on the Persepolitan Pillar bases of Buddha's Walk. The first two are the vowel *a* on the base and its shaft ; the third letter, *k*, was found on the first base of the northern line, opposite *a*. The remaining letters, *g*, *chh*, *j*, and *t*, were found on the 3rd, 7th, 8th, and 11th bases of the same line. The other letters were lost owing to the breaking of the edges or lips of the upper parts of the bases.

VI.—GREAT TEMPLE OF MAHÂBODHI.

The earliest notices that we possess of the *Great Temple* of Mahâbodhi are found in the travels of the Chinese Pilgrims who visited India at various times from the beginning of the 5th century down to the end of the 11th century. The first of these pilgrims was Fa-Hian, who left China in A.D. 399, and travelled across India from the Indus to the sea shore of Orissa, where he embarked for Ceylon, and eventually reached his native country in A.D. 414. The account of his journey has been translated by Remusat, Beal, and Giles. His narrative is brief, and the details, though few, are often interesting and important. His account of Mahâhodhi is unfortunately very meagre; but it is sufficient to show that a Temple of the Bodhi Tree were then standing.[1] His words are, "The sites of the Great Pagodas have always been associated together "from the time of the Nirvâna. The four Great Pagodas are those erected on the place "where he was born, *where he obtained emancipation*, where he began to preach, and "where he entered Nirvâna."

Mr. Giles gives the passage more intelligibly, as follows:—

"From the Nirvâna of Buddha to the present time the sites of the four Great "Pagodas have been handed down (by tradition) without a break."

Laidlay, in his translation of Remusât, has, "The *four great towers erected* in "commemoration of all the holy acts that Fo performed while in the world *are preserved* "*to this moment*."

From this statement it appears to be certain that there was a great Vihâra of the Mahâbodhi Tree in existence at the time of Fa Hian's visit in A.D. 409.

The next pilgrims, Sung Yun and Hoei Seng, visited N. India in A.D. 520, but their travels were confined to the Kabul Valley and Western Panjâb, and are of no use for the present work.

The most valuable works that have come down to us are the Life and Travels of the Pilgrim Hwen Thsang, who left China in A.D. 629, and did not return until A.D. 648. During his long pilgrimage of 19 years he visited most of the principal places in India, and having mastered the Sanskrit language, the details which he gives of the state of the Buddhist religion are particularly full and valuable. His geographical

[1] Beal, p. 124; Giles, p. 78; Laidlay, p. 280.

notices also are important, as he gives the Sanskrit names of most of the places, together with their relative positions, so that most of them have been identified. He frequently also gives the names of the reigning kings, and his account of the powerful king, Harsha Vardhana, is especially valuable.

Hwen Thsang gives a long description of the Mahâbodhi Temple, with numerous measurements and other details, from which it becomes quite clear that the present Temple, in spite of repeated repairs and additions, is actually the same building that was seen by the pilgrim in A.D. 637. He describes it as follows :—

" To the east of the Bodhi Tree there is a Vihâra between 160 and 170 feet in " height, with a base of about 20 paces [or 50 feet]. It is built of bluish bricks, faced " with plaster. It presents several tiers of niches, each of which holds a gilded statue " of Buddha.[1] On all four sides the walls are covered with beautiful sculptures, festoons " of pearls, and figures of Rishis. On its summit there is a gilt copper Amalaka fruit.[2] " Afterwards on the eastern side (or front) there was added a pavilion of two storeys " which presented three stages of projecting roofs. The architraves and pillars, the " doors and the windows, are ornamented with gold and silver chasings, amongst which " pearls and precious stones are inserted. * * * To the right and left of the outer " door there are two large niches, that to the right containing a statue of Avalokiteswara, " and that to the left a statue of Maitreya. Both statues are of silver, and about " 10 feet in height."

This description of the Mahâbodhi Temple, as it stood in A.D. 637, tallies so closely with the Great Temple as it now stands, that, in my opinion, there can be no reasonable doubt that it is, in spite of all its repairs and alterations, the same building which was described by the Chinese pilgrim, as will be seen by the following comparison.

1st. The dimensions of the two Temples are *exactly* the same, the present building being 48 feet square at its base, and between 160 and 170 feet in height. In 1861 my measurement of its height, in its broken state, was 160 feet from the floor of the chamber to the top of the ruined pinnacle. It is now, after repair of the pinnacle, upwards of 170 feet.

2nd. It is built of bluish bricks, with a coating of plaster.

3rd. The four faces present several tiers of niches, rising one above the other, each of which, no doubt, once held a Buddhist figure. Only three figures remained when I first saw the building.

4th. The entrance on the eastern side was certainly an addition to the original building, as its courses of bricks did not correspond with those of the main body of the Temple.

But the discoveries made during the removal of the ruinous buttresses on the west side, or back, of the building were more decisive of the antiquity of the main body of the Temple. On this west face there was a row of 13 niches, each containing a Buddhist figure. Five of these niches were hidden by the addition of the great central buttress, but their statues, their mouldings, and their ornaments, were all left untouched.[3]

---

[1] Mr. Beal, Vol. II., 118, note 69, says, that there is no mention of Buddha, which is in direct opposition to Julien's version, who says, II. 464, that each niche holds " une statuette en or du Buddha."

[2] Julien, II. 464 ; Beal., II. 118.

[3] *See* Plate XII.—Where the back wall has its 13 niches all numbered.

As the concealed statues were all of the Gupta style of sculpture, while those of the buttress itself were all of a much later period, there can be no doubt that this central buttress was an after addition to the original building.

At a still later period two additional small buttresses, F F, were added, one on each side of the central buttress. As each of these covered two niches, there remained in view only two niches of the original wall on each side.

The removal of the great central buttress disclosed the curious fact that it was itself not a single work, but the result of several distinct and separate additions, which were undoubtedly made at different times. As these successive additions throw a flood of light on the history of the Temple, I will now describe them in detail, beginning with the earliest. and working outwards to the latest.

The back wall of the original Temple, with its line of 13 niches, is shown in the lower photograph of Plate XII. In the central niche, No. 7, and in the first niche shown on left hand, Plate XIV., is seen a figure of the Vajrâsan Buddha, seated under the Bodhi Tree, with an attendant holding a *chauri* on each side of him. It still bore traces of red colour when uncovered. This figure, and those in the two niches on each side, are parts of the original work, which was afterwards completely concealed by the addition of the great central buttress. The figures in these niches are quite different in style from those in the other niches, and the brackets of the mouldings above them are also quite different. These differences will be discussed hereafter when I come to speak of the main work of the central buttress. *See* Plate XV. for the mouldings of Lions' heads on the central buttress instead of plain square blocks, as on the main building immediately behind the buttress.

In the photographs already referred to, upper of Plate XIV., there will be seen a second statue of the Vajrâsan Buddha, with his two attendants, in the niche immediately above the central niche. The object of placing these figures over the centre of the back wall must have been to show that here was the famous Vajrâsan Throne. Accordingly right under the figure of Buddha there was found, placed against the wall, a polished Vajrâsan Throne of grey sandstone, 7 feet 10½ inches long by 4 feet 7½ inches broad, and 6¼ inches thick. The whole surface was carved with geometrical patterns, circular in the middle, with a double border of squares.[1] All the four outer faces of the slab were richly carved with pigeons and the conventional acanthus flowers and the geese of Asoka's Pillar Capitals. A view of the south side is given in Plate XIII. As the back edge of the slab, which abutted against the wall, was also carved, it would seem that it did not occupy its original position, and I believe that it must once have formed the upper slab of the Sandstone Throne which was found *inside* Asoka's Temple.[2]

---

[1] *See* Plate X. for a specimen.

[2] These tables, or platform slabs, were placed under the Bodhi Trees for the reception of the offerings of flowers. They are still in use in Ceylon, of which we have a striking example in the erection of a white marble slab in front of the Bodhi Tree at Mahâbodhi by a pilgrim from Ceylon so late as A.D. 1884. The slab was presented by Edmund Gunaratna, of Colombo, as noted in the inscription on its upper surface as follows:—

BUDDHAWASSE

2427

Mâgasira mâsa punnama guruwâre Lankâdipe Pedrika Ilangakon iti vissuta Mahâ mantini Pamukhâname haccânan Buddhopâsakananga Atta naca mûlavya Karanena Gâlupure invasatâ Buddha Gaya manuppatena Edmund Goonaratne Kolambapure vâsala mudali Raja macca Durandharena mayâ Bhagavato jaya. Mahâbodhi pûjâya patitthâpitani pupphâsananciti.

The date of ***Buddhavarsha*** is the Ceylonese reckoning from the Nirvâna in B.C. 543 = A.D. 1884.

This outer Vajrâsan slab rested on a brick platform 3 feet 4 inches in height, which was ornamented with boldly moulded figures of men and lions of very early work.[1] From the round faces, the full lips, and easy pose of the figures, with all of which features I have long been familiar in the Sârnâth sculptures, I have no hesitation in assigning this pedestal to the time of the later Indo-Scythians and earlier Guptas. This date is corroborated by the characters of the inscription, which is carved on the narrow edges of the upper surface. Unfortunately all that remains of this inscription is so much injured that very little can be read consecutively. The words *patimâ patithapat*, "statue established," followed by *Mâtapita*, "father and mother," are distinct, and as they form a common portion of most Indo-Scythian inscriptions, I conclude that this outer Vajrâsan slab must have been placed in its present position during the flourishing period of their rule in northern India and the Panjâb. This, then, must be the real date of the Great Temple itself, a conclusion which is still further corroborated by the two following discoveries, made inside and outside the Temple.

1st. On removing the plaster facing of the inner Vajrâsan Throne there was discovered in the middle of the front face, and just below the sandstone floor, and resting on the upper plastered floor, a ball of stiff earth or clay, which on being broken yielded the following relics. *See* Plate XXII.

Gold—2 impressions in thin gold of the obverse face of a gold coin of Huvishka, joined together, and held by a ring.
- 1 Crescent of thin gold, 0·6 inch broad.
- 4 Flowers, 0·75 inch, with a pale sapphire in centre of each.
- 3 Shells, 0·6 inch long.
- 4 Kamarak fruits, 0·2 inch broad.
- 5 Buttons, or knobs, 0·45 inch broad.
- 26 large discs, 37·5 grains, or 1·44 each.
- 29 small discs, 11 grains, 0·38 each.

Silver—5 punch-marked coins, one with human figures, besides many small shapeless fragments.
- 1 thin hemisphere.
- 27 large discs.
- 14 small discs.

Gems—145 *Pearls*, small, all black with age.
- *Coral*, pale; about 3 Table spoons of bits and several coral shell ornaments.
- *Crystal*, numerous fragments, all uncut.
- *Sapphires*, small fragments, valueless.
- *Rubies*, small fragments, valueless.
- *Emeralds*, small fragments, valueless.

Afterwards it was found, on minute examination, that all the remains of plaster taken off the Sandstone Throne contained small fragments of pounded coral, sapphire, crystal,

---

[1] *See* Plate XIII. for a view.

pearl, &c., of which as much as a basket full was collected. In fact the mortar, instead of being composed of sand and lime, consisted of coarsely pounded coral mixed with small fragments of sapphire, crystal, pearl, and ivory, bound together with lime.

The early date of this deposit is attested by the presence of the five punch-marked silver coins, which would point to a date as early as the 2nd or 3rd century A.D.; when these coins were still current. The gold impressions also of Huvishka's coin would seem to point to the period of his reign as the actual time when the deposit was made, or about 120 to 160 A.D.

2nd. Another corroboration of this date is derived from an inscription on the pedestal of a statue of Buddha which was found near a small ruined Temple close to the South gate of the Railing of the Great Temple.[1] The early date of this statue is attested by the unmistakeable Indo-Scythian or Gupta style of the letters and sculptures; but as the inscription is dated in the Samvat year 64, and the record is worded in the usual form of the Indo-Scythian inscriptions found at Mathura, I have no doubt that it belongs to the 2nd century of the Christian era. In another place I have given my reasons for reckoning the dates of Indo-Scythian inscriptions by the Seleukidan era, by omitting the hundreds. In the present case the date of 64 would represent 464 of the Seleukidan era, equivalent to 152 A.D., which, as it agrees with the ascertained dates of Huvishka's reign, may be accepted as the actual date of the building of the Temple in which the statue was enshrined.[2]

This inscription is unfortunately very much broken, and the name of the donor of the statue is not quite clear. He was a Mahârâja himself, and may therefore have been the agent employed by the Indo-Scythian King Huvishka in building the Great Temple. His name was either *Tukamâla* or *Turamâla*.

As these three evidences of the antiquity of the Temple all agree in pointing to the reign of the Indo-Scythian King Huvishka as the period when the Great Temple was erected, I am inclined to think that he may have furnished the funds, while the actual builder was the Brahman mentioned by Hwen Thsang, who must also be identified with the *Penthagu-gyi* of the Burmese inscription.

The Burmese term *Penthagu* is said by Hla-Oung to be a common term for a pious layman who is zealous in propagating his religion. It is therefore the exact equivalent of the Sanskrit *Upâsika*, which was the title of a "pious Buddhist not in orders." It seems also very probable that as the Burmese pronounce the letter *S* as a soft *th*, the term *Penthagu* may be only a corrupt form of *Upâsika* by dropping the initial letter *U*.

In Ratna Pâlas' translation of the Burmese inscription, which gives a brief history of the Temple, it is said that it was rebuilt by a priest named *Naikmahanta*, but both Colonel Burney and Hla Oung call him *Penthagu-gyi*. As *Naik Mahant* means simply the Chief Priest or Great Abbot, and as *gyi* means "great" in Burmese, the term *Penthagugyi* may perhaps be referred to *Mahâ-Upâsika*.

According to Hwen Thsang, the builder of the Great Temple was a Brahman, "who "was not a believer in Buddha, and sacrificed to Maheswara." After his conversion he

[1] *See* Plate XXV. for Statue and Inscription.

[2] If the date be referred to the Saka Samvat, then the year 64 added to 78 A.D. will give A.D. 142 as the date of the statue.

built a large Vihâra by the Bodhi Tree, while his younger brother dug a tank, which must be the present *Budhokhar*, or *Buddha-pokhar*, to the south of the Great Temple. "The Brahman then became the great Minister of the king."

Now there is a story told by Târanâth of two Upâsika brothers, named *Mudgaragâmini* and *Sankara*, who founded the famous monastery of Nâlanda. The date is given as shortly before the appearance of Nâgârjuna.

Hwen Thsang calls the founder of the Nâlanda Monastery *Sho-kia-lo-o-tie-to*, which both Julien and Beal render by Sakrâditya, in accordance with the Chinese translation "le soleil de l'empereur." But as there would seem to be some connection between the two Brahman brothers who built the Mahâbodhi Temple and these two brothers who founded the Nâlanda Monastery, I think it probable that the name of *Sankara* given by Târanâth may be the correct one. Hwen Thsang himself says that the Mahâbodhi Brahman was a worshipper of Siva which accords with Siva's name of Sankara, and not with the title of Sakra or Indra. The date given for the foundation of the Nâlanda Monastery agrees very well with that which I have assigned for the Mahâbodhi Temple, as Nâgârjuna is believed to have lived about the 2nd century A.D.

With regard to the style of the Great Temple of Mahâbodhi, we have the distinct testimony of Hwen Thsang himself that the Temple of Bâlâditya at Nâlanda resembled the Great Vihâra built under the Bodhi Tree in magnificence, in size, and in the style of the enshrined statue. Now the lower part (about one-third) of the Great Temple at Nâlanda is still standing, and we are thus able to compare the two Temples with one another. The similarity of plan, as well as of style, is very striking. In the statement about the dimensions there is a discrepancy in the height of the Nâlanda Temple which in the Travels is said to be 300 feet, whereas in the Life of Hwen Thsang it is only 200 feet. The latter number agrees sufficiently well for comparison with that of the Mahâbodhi Temple, which was from 160 to 170 feet. As I have already pointed out,[1] the proportions of the Nâlanda Temple agree exactly with those of the Mahâbodhi Temple. The base of the tower of the Nâlanda Temple is 63 feet square, while that of Mahâbodhi is nearly 50 feet. If the same proportions were observed in the former Temple its height would have been just about 200 feet, as stated by Hwen Thsang.

As a last corroboration of the early date which I have assigned to the Mahâbodhi Temple, I can point to the inscriptions on the inner side of the copings, or architraves, of the surrounding Railing. As the lines of the present Railing are parallel to the walls of the Great Temple, and not to the lines of Buddha's Walk, and the Asoka Temple, it is certain that the Railing must have been re-arranged, and considerably extended. The old enclosure of Asoka was only 250 feet in extent, with 64 Pillars, whereas the circuit of the present Railing is not less than 520 feet, which would have required just double the number of Pillars. There are the remains of 62 Pillars now in situ, of which a large number are of granite, and the remainder of fine sandstone. As there are about 20 more of these Pillars still in the various courts of the Mahant's dwelling, besides three taken to Kensington, and three or four to Calcutta, the full number still existing may be set down as somewhere about 100, which is very near the actual number of 108 required for the whole extent of the present enclosure.

---

[1] *See* Archæological Survey of India, vol. III., 94.

The inscription on the inner side of the coping stone offers another corroboration of the early date of the period of the later Indo-Scythians, or early Guptas. Many of the letters of this inscription are very faint, and the copy given in Plate XXVII. is taken from a paper impression with the letters restored. Some of them may be doubtful, but the greater part of them seem pretty certain. I give the reading of the letters as they appear to me.

1.—. . . kârito yantra *Vajrâsana* vrihad *Gandhakuti* prâsâda murddha vriddhi saraṣataissadhrili prakarmmye punâlamdaikah tagekana * ridapratuda cha d . viharmi chandrârkkatârakam Bhagavate Buddhâ yaddegaradânenaghu ka prudimaḥ Swakârîsahamrisâde vaga . . Bha . tita pratisa mâdhane . ddrati mayam cha pratihamghṛita pradipargu ṣata dineni parâine karitaḥ Vihârepi Bhagavaterotya *Buddha pratimâ* . . .

2.—. . . . ṇagradipâkshaya siti . . kah . Vihâraipi . Ṣubha . kâri . . . . . bha . . . . . . viha . . . . itaṁ davaga pradeṣi chatarana . . . . . vibharami . . . paghu . ka isyaḥ payomaya masante madhuram anya sitpante dine purvvam châ prahata kakshetu matpâditamtade tatsarvvam yaumarya punya prachite sambhâram tana mitrsḥ . . .

I see the names of *Vajrâsana*, *Gandhakuti*, and *Vihâra*, and also of *Bhagavata Buddha* and the statue of Buddha (*Buddha pratima*) in the first line, "all of which will "last as long as the Moon, Sun, and Stars" (*Chandrârkkatârakam*). I see also the mention of clarified butter for lamps (*ghritapradipo*) which was read by Dr. Rajendra Lâl.

The second of these coping inscriptions is a very short one, and is probably, as suggested by Dr. Rajenda Lâl, only the work of a pilgrim recording a gift of money (*ṭanka*) apparently for the supply of lamps. It is rather rudely engraved. As it cannot be of later date than the 4th or 5th century, the coping must have been still in situ when the record was cut upon it.

VII.—ADDITIONS AND RESTORATIONS.

The first addition made to the Temple on the outside was a new figure of Buddha, A. which was built upon the top of the Vajrâsan Throne, immediately in front of the central niche, No. 7, containing the original Vajrâsan Buddha, which it completely concealed.[1] This new figure is shown in the lower photograph of Plate XIV. It was about twice the size of the old statue, and had a distinct pedestal of its own, which rested on the back part of the Vajrâsan stone. This pedestal had three niches in front, each containing a human figure. These niches were at first separated by small pilasters with bevelled edges, which were afterwards turned into *vajras* or thunderbolts. At what time the new figure of Buddha was added, may, I think, be fixed at about A.D. 300 to 400, as a copper coin of Pasupati, Raja of Nepâl, was found in its stomach. This coin was of the Bull and Crescent type as given in Plate XXII., fig. 1. A similar coin of Pasupati was found in a small stupa outside the north-east corner of the enclosure. Along with the coin there was a very thin saucer, 2¾ inches in diameter and 1 inch deep, and also a thin iron vessel, 4 inches in diameter, with a projecting edge cut into vandykes. These two vessels contained the following relics :—

37 pieces of crystal, some broken, some hollowed out.
7 cornelian beads.
19 Lapis-lazuli beads.
30 glass beads.
3 red Jasper beads.
4 garnets.
1 large bead of black stone, polished.
1 small pearl, discoloured.
1 small bit of gold.
13 bits of mother-of-pearl.
2 Jacinth.
1 Amethyst.

In addition to these objects, but quite separate from them, there were two small copper plates, each inscribed with the Buddhist creed in mediæval characters of about the 7th or 8th century.[2] As these were placed apart from the relics, they could not

[1] *See* lower part of Plate XII., where the original figure in the middle niche is uncovered. *See also* Plate XIV., upper photograph, left-hand niche. In the Plan of the Temple, Plate XI., the outer Vajrâsan Throne is marked V2, and the position of the new figure of Buddha is shown by a thick black line on the east side of the slab against the back wall of the Temple.

[2] Plate XXIV., figs. 3 and 4.

have belonged to the original deposit of Pasupatis' time. The very letters of their inscriptions show that they must have been at least four centuries later. They may have been inserted when some repairs were made to the statue at the time when the plaster front with its five pilasters was given to the pedestal covering up the old Vajrâsan front.

G. About the same time there was added to the outer face of the Vajrâsan a granite front of squared stones, marked by a black line, G. in Plan, to west of the Vajrâsan slab. Its remains may be seen in the lower photograph of Plate XIV., immediately in front of the Vajrâsan slab.

H.H. At some subsequent period, *see* Plate XI., a solid square pier was built on each side of the Vajrâsan Throne; that to the north completely covering up Nos. 5 and 6 niches, and that to the south covering up Nos. 8 and 9 niches. The interval in front of the new statue on the Vajrâsan was, perhaps, arched over to form a niche for the figure.

N. The great opening was afterwards filled up solid, with a facing of small niches on the west side. I suppose these two works G. and HH. to belong to the time shortly preceding Raja Pûrna Varma. When the Pipal Tree had been entirely uprooted by Sasângka, and the figure of Buddha inside the Temple concealed by a wall built by his minister, I conclude that the figure of the Vajrâsan Buddha outside the Temple must have been concealed in the same way by building up the niche nearly solid. This would have taken place about 600 to 620 A.D., shortly before Hwen Thsang's visit. This wall is marked N.

E.E. At a later date, another massive addition was made to the buttress, forming a great niche in the middle, the remains of which are well shown in the upper photograph of Plate XII. The west facing of this work formed a grand entrance of richly carved basalt, of which only the sill now remains. From its style I judge it to belong to the 10th or 11th century, when the use of fine basalt became common. This work I believe to have been done by the Burmese, between A.D. 1035 and 1086.

F.F. The last addition consisted of two square buttresses, one on each side of the great central buttress. These two works were built entirely of good bricks and lime mortar, and their lower mouldings did not coincide with those of the old Temple and the central buttress.[1] This work was probably executed by some of the later Pâla Kings in the 12th century, when the great central buttress had shown signs of yielding to the pressure of the roots of the holy Pipal Tree above.

P. I have already mentioned the great addition that was made to the front of the Temple, as described by Hwen Thsang. But we have now acquired some further information about this work by the discovery of a small mediæval model of the Temple in stone, of which four views are given in Plate XVI., with a plan of the model placed beside an actual plan of the building for comparison. From this model we see that the holy Pipal Tree had already been placed on the top of the basement immediately behind the Temple. We see also in front an open Hall or Portico, with four Pillars in the lower storey or basement, and a lofty portico above, with a sloping arched roof.

---

[1] *See* the Photograph of Plate XII.

We see also the remains of some corner towers, of which traces still existed on the terrace itself in our days. The plan of the Tower marked T, and shaded in Plate XI., was quite distinct on the terraced level of the basement on the S.W.

The whole of this Portico was in a very ruinous state; but the side Pillars or Pilasters still remained in situ. One of the central Pillars was found close by, and a portion of the second Pillar is now in Calcutta.

The style of these Pillars is the same as that of the Pillars of the Toran, which formed the entrance Gateway on the east; and also the same as those of the portico of the Great Temple at Nâlanda. This last was also an after addition, as I have shown several years ago.[1] In this case, however, the addition was a new stone basement built against the brick Temple, where, as at Mahâbodhi, the addition was of brick.

In his translation of Hwen Thsang's account of this eastern pavilion, Mr. Beal apparently makes it a part of the original building.[2] His words are:—"The eastern "face adjoins a storeyed pavilion, the projecting eaves of which rise one over the other "to the height of three distinct chambers." In this passage he has left out the important words *à la suite,* which are given by Julien.[3] "Du côté de l'est, on a "construit, *à la suite,* un pavillon à deux étages, dont les *toits saillants s'élèvent* "*sur trois raugs.*" I have no means of testing the accuracy of these translations, but I am able to say, from actual examination, that the eastern pavilion certainly was an addition to the original building. As it was made before the time of Hwen Thsang, I think that it may be assigned to the Prince whom the Burmese inscription calls Thado Mang, or King Sado, most probably about A.D. 400, when it would appear that there was much activity at Mahâbodhi, as several of the small Stûpas yielded coins of Pasupati, Raja of Nepâl.

Some alterations and additions must have been made by Raja Pûrna Varma, about A.D. 600 to 620, shortly before the time of Hwen Thsang. The holy Pipal Tree had been completely destroyed by Sasângka; and, in spite of Hwen Thsang's statement about the escape of the great statue of Buddha inside, I have no doubt that both statue and Throne were destroyed at the same time. To Pûrna Varma, therefore, I would ascribe the erection of the blue basalt pedestal in front of the inner Throne, and the vaulting of the inner chamber, which rested on the same floor as the blue pedestal, and was therefore not a part of the original work. Outside we know that he surrounded the new Bodhi Tree with a stone wall 24 feet high, which in Hwen Thsang's time was still 20 feet high.[4] The difference of level I would explain by a great influx of sand, which actually hid the outer Vajrâsan at the time of Hwen Thsang's visit.[5] This sand was probably deposited by a flood of the River Nairanjan. In January 1872 I found no less than 2 feet 8 inches of sand between the gateway Pillars outside the great buttress at the back of the Temple. Upon this sand there was laid a strong terraced floor of lime mortar, 2 inches thick, which reached up to the top of the lowest Rail-bar of the Railings. During the late excavations this terraced floor was found to extend in all

---

1 Archæological Survey, Vol. III., Pl. XXXI., figs. 11 and 12.
2 Beal's Si-yu-ki, II., 118.
3 Julien's Hwen Thsang, II., 465.
4 Beal's Si-yu-ki, II., 118, and Julien's Hwen Thsang, II., 464.
5 Julien, II., 461, "et il n'est possible de le voir."

directions, and on the outer side of the northern Railing it was found resting upon sand up to the top of the lowest Rail-bar. Inside the Railing the sand must have been cleared away from Buddha's Walk, as Hwen Thsang notes that the walk was 3 feet high. During the recent excavations it was found that the top of the Walk was just on the same level as the terraced floor which rested on the sand.

The work done by the Burmese in the 11th century would appear to have been a complete repair and restoration of the whole building, from the floor to the top of the pinnacle. We now possess two inscriptions which refer to their work; both are dated, and we thus obtain two trustworthy records of the age of the Burmese restoration.

The first of these inscriptions is engraved on a copper-gilt umbrella, which was found by Mr. Beglar carefully buried 8 feet under the modern ground level, to the west of the Temple at the spot marked by a star (*) in Plate XVIII. The inscription is repeated in mediæval Nâgari characters just below the Burmese record.[1] The Burmese portion is much injured, but I can still read the name of *Sri Dhamma Guru* in it. The Indian inscription, which is nearly perfect, opens as follows :—

"*Sam* 397, *Sri Dharma Raja Guru.*"

Here the date, which is very clearly carved, can only be referred to the Burmese common era of A.D. 638, which fixes the period of Dharma Raja Guru's visit to 638 + 397 = A.D. 1035.

The other Burmese inscription was found by the Burmese Mission under Colonel Burney; it is inscribed on a stone slab, and was discovered fixed in a wall of the Mahant's residence. There I saw it in January 1862. Three translations of it have been published,—1st, by Ratna Pâla, a Singhalese Pali scholar; 2nd, by Colonel Burney; and, 3rd, by Mr. Hla Oung, a Burmese scholar. The inscription professes to record a history of the original building and the successive repairs of the Temple.[2] Two dates are given in figures, accompanied in each case by the day of the week as well as the day of the month. The following is a brief abstract of this valuable record :—

1. Asoka built the first Temple.
2. Temple rebuilt by Naik Mahanta.
3. Temple restored by Raja Sado-Meng.
4. Raja Sempyu-Sakhen-tara-Mengyi deputed his Guru, Sri Dhamma Râja-Guna, to superintend the restoration of the Temple : work not completed.
5. Varadasi Naik Thera petitioned the Raja to undertake the work, which was then entrusted to "the younger Pyu-Sakheng" and his minister, Ratha.

This last work was begun in the Sakka Raj year 441, on *Friday* the 10th of Pyadola, and finished in 448, on Sunday the 8th of Tachung-mangla (or Tasoung-mong).

Here I have given my own reading of the dates as 441 and 448 for the following reasons :—

The inscription on the gilt-copper umbrella shows that the Burmese Mission under Dharma Raja Guru came to India near the close of the 4th Burmese century; and as the longer Burmese inscription shows that the repairs were completed by the younger

[1] *See* Plate XXIX. for a view of this Umbrella and its inscriptions.

[2] For Ratna Pala's translation, and for Colonel Burney's translation, and for Hla Oung's translation, *see* Babu Rajendra's Buddha Gaya.

Pyu Sakheng not long afterwards, it follows that this second inscription must be dated in the 5th century of the Burmese era, and not in the 7th century, as hitherto read. I therefore read the two dates of this inscription as 441 and 448, in preference to the very much later dates of 667 and 668, which had been generally adopted previously. I have tested all the possible readings of these dates as 641, 647, 661, 667, 648, and 668 by the week days mentioned in the inscription. Not one of them stands this test; whereas the two dates of 441 and 448, which I have adopted, do actually agree with the week days mentioned in the inscription. The evidence in favour of my readings is therefore doubly strong. The two dates noted in this inscription correspond, according to my calculation, with the following European dates:—

1. Sakka-râj year 441, *Friday*, 10th of Pyadola, was *Friday*, 6th December, A.D. 1079.
2. Sakka-râj year 448, *Sunday*, 8th of Tachung Mungla, was *Sunday*, 18th October, A.D. 1086.

These readings of the dates allow a period of six years and ten months for the complete restoration of the Temple, instead of the very short period of only 10 months allowed by the former readings.

It is difficult to state exactly all the different portions of the work done by the Burmese; but the following appear to me to be quite certain:—

1. Complete repair and restoration of all the walls, including stucco facing.

2. Complete renewal of the pinnacle of the Temple. This is proved by the discovery of a short Burmese inscription on one of the bricks of the conventional *amalaka* fruit or crenellated wheel of the pinnacle. Several other bricks were also inscribed with short records in Bengali letters of two lines. These latter read simply *Gopapâle* and *Dharma-Sinhe*, which are believed to be simply masons' names.[1]

3. The addition of the two side buttresses to the right and left of the great central buttress, containing the great cell, is, perhaps, a later work. These were built with good lime mortar, similar to that used in the pinnacle just described. It seems certain, therefore, that these two works belong to much about the same period. That the great repairs of the Temple were done in the mediæval period is, I think, clearly shown by the *terra-cotta* figure which was found in one of the top niches on the east side of the Temple, as the letters of its two inscribed seals belong to the 10th or 11th century. This figure is now in the British Museum.

From the length of time taken by the Burmese in making their repairs, I have no doubt that their work embraced the complete restoration of the whole building. I suppose that the masons, who, as I have just said, must have been chiefly Bengâlis, did not scruple to alter the style and character of the mouldings, but only in their details, while they left all the principal features of the architecture unchanged.

The photograph of the north end of the great buttress, in Plate XV., shows decisively the extent and nature of the changes made in the repairs of the great lines of

---

[1] *See* Plate XXIX. for these masons' names in Bengâli and Burmese. As these are both Hindu names, we have a proof that Hindu masons must have been employed in making the repairs. Of course the great mass of the workmen must have been Hindus, although it is not improbable that the Burmese agent may have brought over some head masons to superintend the repairs.

moulding. The buttress having been forcibly pushed outwards by the roots of the Holy Tree, the bold mouldings above the lowest line of niches were exposed to view, and have been preserved in the photograph. The original mouldings consisted of a double line of plain dentils, above which was a long line of bold circular flowers cut in brick. On the buttress itself, and on the remaining exposed niches of the main building, the row of flowers was changed into a line of small Vandykes, or half diamonds. The upper row of dentils was changed into a line of lions' heads, with garlands suspended from mouth to mouth, while the lower row of dentils was changed into a line of alternate dumpy pilasters and squatted human figures.

But the alterations were apparently confined to the mouldings and ornaments, while all the main features of the building remained unchanged. The tiers of niches, the round and fluted angles of the corners, were all intact, where they still existed; but the flowered ornaments and the petty details of the pilasters were different. The dado panels beneath the niches, which were originally diapered with two rows of plain, sunken squares, were changed to flat panels of rich foliated ornament. So far back as 1871 I had already noticed these alterations in the style of the mouldings. (*See* Archæological Survey of India, III., p. 104, and Plate XXXI.)

During the course of the next century, A.D. 1100 to 1200, several works were carried on under the superintendence of a zealous Buddhist priest, Dharma Rakshita, at the cost of Asokaballa, Raja of Sapâdalaksha. No less than four inscriptions of this prince have been found, of which three are dated, namely, two in the Bengali era of Lakshmana Sena, and the third in the Parinirvâna of Buddha. Pandit Bhagwân Lâl has identified Sapâdalaksha with the hill country of Siwâlik, including Kumâun and Garhwâl. But, according to the first Muhammadan authors, Hânsi was the capital of Siwâlik, which then included the whole of Northern Rajputâna down to Sâmbhar and Mandor of Jodhpur. Ajmer was another capital of Sapâdalaksha.

VII.—BODHI-TREE.

The earliest description of the famous Pipal Tree under which Sâkya Sinha sat for six years until he obtained emancipation is given by Hwen Thsang.[1] He says: "The "Bodhi Tree above the everlasting Throne, is the same as the Pippal Tree. In old days "when Buddha was alive, it was several hundred feet high. Although it has often been "injured by cutting, it still is 40 or 50 feet in height. Buddha sitting under this tree "reached perfect wisdom, and therefore it is called the 'Tree of Knowledge' [*Bodhi-"drûma.*] The bark is of a yellowish-white colour, the leaves and twigs of a dark "green." It was the custom in his time to bathe the roots with scented water and perfumed milk, a practice which I have witnessed at the present day.

The Bodhi Tree was first cut down by Asoka himself, and, on its miraculous restoration, it was again cut down by Asoka's Queen. Once more it was miraculously restored, and the pilgrim makes no further mention of its destruction until the time of Raja Ṣaṣângka, who cut it down and dug up the roots. He then "burnt it with fire, and "sprinkled it with the juice of the sugar cane, desiring to destroy it entirely, and not "leave a trace of it behind." Some months afterwards Raja Pûrna Varma revived the roots of the Tree with the milk of a thousand cows, and in a single night it sprang up again to a height of 10 feet. Then, fearing that the Tree might once more be cut down, Pûrna Varma surrounded it with a wall of stone 24 feet in height, which in Hwen Thsang's time was still about 20 feet high.[2] This restoration must have taken place about A.D. 600 to 620, after the power of Ṣaṣângka had been humbled by Harsha Vardhana.

Both Mr. Beglar and myself agree in thinking that the surrounding of the Tree with this high wall refers to the placing of the new Tree on the terrace of the Temple, which is rather more than 30 feet above the original ground level.

The next description of the Tree is that given by Dr. Buchanan in 1811. He says, "The Tree is in full vigour, and cannot in all probability exceed 100 years in age; but a "similar one may have existed in the same place, when the Temple was entire."[3]

In December 1862, I found this Tree "very much decayed; one large stem to the "westward, with three branches, was still green, but the other branches were barkless "and rotten."[4] I next saw the Tree in 1871, and again in 1875, when it had become completely decayed, and shortly afterwards, in 1876, the only remaining portion of the Tree fell over the west wall during a storm, and the Old Pipal Tree was gone. Many seeds, however, had been collected, and young scions of the parent tree were already in existence to take its place.

---

[1] Beal's Si-yu-ki, II., 116. [2] Beal's Si-yu-ki, II., 118. [3] Eastern India, I., 76.

[4] Archæological Survey, I., 5. The photographs taken about this time by Mr. Peppe show the tree in the last stage of decay.

Afterwards in 1880, when I saw the Vajrâsan Throne uncovered outside the back wall of the Temple, it struck me that possibly some trace of the old Bodhi Trees might still be found where the original Tree must have stood. I, therefore, had the ground dug up at a short distance to the west of the Vajrâsan Throne. In the sandy soil, just outside the granite facing of the Throne, 3 feet below the level of the foot of the Throne, and 30 feet below the terrace level where the modern Tree had stood, I found two large pieces of an Old Pipal Tree, one 6½ inches in length, and the other 4 inches. As the whole mass of the great buttress at the back of the Temple, 32 feet long and 30 feet high by 14 feet thick, had been standing over this spot for more than 12 centuries, it seems not improbable that these two fragments may be part of the Pipal Tree which was cut down by Şaşângka about A.D. 600 to 620.

The story of the destruction of the Tree by Tishya Rakshita, the Queen of Asoka, is differently told in the Asoka Avadâna, but the result is the same.[1]

No doubt the Bodhi Tree was often cut down, although we have so few notices of such a catastrophe. Târânâth records an invasion of Magadha by the Western King, Hunimanta, apparently about the 1st century A.D.[2] As the Temples are said to have been destroyed, the Canopied Walk must have been thrown down and destroyed, and the famous Bodhi Tree could not have escaped. It seems to have been spared during the latter end of the 7th century, after the death of Harsha Vardhana had left the country in the power of the Brahmans under Aditya Sena and his successors. During their time the Mahâbodhi was repeatedly visited by Chinese pilgrims, all of whom mention the Bodhi Tree as still standing. If it escaped during the following century, 700 to 800 A.D., the Tree planted by Pûrna Varmma may have lasted down to the time of the Buddhist dynasty of Pâla Kings, which began to reign about A.D. 813. After this it was safe until the time of the Muhammadan invasion under Bakhtiyâr Khalji in A.D. 1201. As the Moslems spared the famous Tree at Peshâwar, it is probable that the Mahâbodhi Tree was then left untouched.

As the Pipal is a quick growing and short-lived Tree, there must have been a long succession of fresh trees raised from seed, from the time of Asoka down to the present day; perhaps as many as twelve or fifteen, or even twenty, to meet the frequent destruction to which it was exposed.

In the Burmese chronicles it is stated that King Pasenadi (Prasenajit) surrounded the Bodhi Tree with a double wall, and that a third wall was added by Dharm-Asoka.[3] If this account can be accepted, I would suggest that the double enclosure of Prasenajit must have been only a double palisade of wood, which would have been much decayed during the two centuries and a half which intervened between the two monarchs. I conclude, also, that it would have been altogether removed when Asoka built his Temple immediately to the east of the Bodhi Tree.

---

[1] *See* Babu Rajendra Lâl's Buddha Gaya, p. 97.

[2] Vassilief's Târânâth, by La Comme, p. 51, note. Hunimanta is said to have conquered Magadha, and destroyed the temples. I suspect, however, that *Hunimanta* may have been *Mihirkul,* King of the *Hûnas,* or White Huns.

[3] Bigandet, "Life of Gaudama."

IX.—TORAN GATEWAY.

At 78 feet to the east of the Great Temple, and 54 feet from the Bluestone Railing, there was formerly a massive Toran Gateway. In November 1879, shortly after the Burmese had been clearing the courtyard, I found a single pillar of large dimensions, just inside the south pillar of the Burmese Gateway. From its position I judged that it might have formed one of the pillars of a Toran Gateway, leading up to the Temple. This opinion was confirmed by the discovery of two large four-bracket capitals, which corresponded in size with the top of the shaft, which was happily still unbroken. Sometime afterwards the second pillar was found by Mr. Beglar, during the clearance excavations for drainage, near the north pillar of the Burmese Gateway. This furnished a complete confirmation of my opinion as to the former existence of a Toran Gateway near this position. On seeing the direction in which this last pillar was lying, I searched near its base for some traces of the foundation of the Gateway. My search was almost immediately successful, as I soon found a foundation 15 feet long by 6 feet broad, with a large square stone let in near each end, on each face of which there were two socket holes for the reception of iron cramps. On examining the foot of the shaft, it was found that it had the same number of socket holes on each side, and at exactly the same distances apart. Mr. Beglar then pointed out a long massive beam, which, on measurement, was found to be the architrave of the Toran.

The shafts of the pillars are $14\frac{1}{2}$ feet high, 2 feet 1 inch square at base, and 1 foot $3\frac{1}{2}$ inches square at top. The bracket capitals had a square centre of $15\frac{1}{2}$ inches, with two oblong branches, and two short branches of $11\frac{1}{2}$ inches. They were 16 inches in height, thus making the clear height of the Toran nearly 17 feet. *See* Plate XVII.

The capitals were ornamented both on their faces and on their sides. The decoration of the shafts consisted of several bands of simple ornament, gradually changing from the plain square dado to octagonal, then to sixteen-sided and to circular. The whole of the ornamentation is similar to that of the pillars of the portico of the Great Nâlanda Temple, which I have shown from the masons' inscriptions on the stones of the basement to be of the Gupta period, as well as an addition to the original brick building. These Toran pillars are also similar to those of the portico of the Mahâbodhi itself, and as this portico was an addition to the original building, made before the time of Hwen Thsang, it cannot be later than the middle of the 6th century. I think, therefore, that there can be little doubt that this Toran Gateway, as well as the porticoes of the Mahâbodhi and Nâlanda Temples, must date from about the 4th or 5th century A.D. The pillars of all three are made of granite from the same quarry.

In Plate XVII. will be found a view of the Toran Gateway as now set up on its old foundations. The architrave on the top was found by Mr. Beglar on the spot, and as its dimensions agree exactly with the inter-columniation of the two pillars, there can be no doubt that it belonged to the Toran. The distance from centre to centre of the pillars is 10 feet 4 inches, and the clear roadway between them is 8 feet 3 inches, which differs by only 5 inches from the width of the northern and southern Gateways of the surrounding railing. But as these Toran pillars have a great slope, the clear width between them at 5 feet above the ground, is 8 feet 6 inches.

At the same spot were exhumed several kneeling figures, with hands joined in adoration. They may have belonged to the Toran, but I do not see to what parts they could have been attached. Wherever they were placed they must have faced the Temple. There certainly were statues fixed on the east and west sides of the pillars, as there are shallow hollows for their reception, and several socket holes for cramps to keep them in position. The kneeling figures are in the act of performing *Shikko*, as now practised in Burmah. Similar figures are represented on many of the granite pavement stones sketched in outline only. Their date is certain, as the Samvat years are recorded in their inscriptions. But the statues carved in the round are apparently of much earlier date. A good sketch of one of them will be found in Dr. Rajendra's Buddha Gayâ, Plate XIII., fig. 5. I have seen many similar figures in Burma, and I think that the few specimens now existing at Mahâbodhi may be assigned to the time of the Burmese repairs, in the 11th century.

X.—MONUMENTS IN COURTYARD.

According to Hwen Thsang "the sacred monuments inside the enclosure of the "Temple, both Stûpas and Vihâras, were so numerous that they seemed to touch each "other.[1] Kings, princes, and other great men who had embraced the doctrine of "Buddha, built these monuments to preserve his memory." The truth of this statement will be seen by a glance at Plate XVIII., in which only the numerous remains of the lower levels have been conserved. Many others were mere heaps of ruins.[2] Several of the remaining structures are the very monuments that were seen by Hwen Thsang, as all the ruined monuments of a later age were nearly or altogether obliterated by the removal of the bricks and stones, partly by the villagers, and partly by the levelling operations of the last Burmese mission.

All the principal monuments that now remain are marked in the accompanying plate by letters of the alphabet, which generally give the initial of the name of the building. Several of them have been identified from their positions with those described by Hwen Thsang. A few are known by the inscriptions which have been found in them, but the greater number of the smaller Temples and Stûpas are unknown. Many of the Stûpas contained clay seals, but only a few yielded anything that could help to declare their age. One of them, which contained a copper coin of Raja Pasupati, King of Nepâl, must have been built about A.D. 300 to 400. I will begin my account of these monuments with those that are mentioned by Hwen Thsang, adhering to the order in which he places them.

AA are the basements of two old Temples to the right and left of the eastern entrance of the Temple. These I take to be the remains of the two Temples containing the two figures of Avalokiteswara, both seated, and looking eastwards. At the time of the pilgrim's visit the southern and right hand figure was buried up to the breast, and old people then said that "as soon as the figures of this Bodhisatwa sink in the ground and disappear, the law of Buddha will come to an end.[3] The fact that the south

---

1 Julien's Hwen Thsang, II., 460. Beal's Si-yü-ki, II., 115–127.

2 Plate XIX. gives a good view of these monuments, now standing in the north-west portion of the courtyard. All of these were buried deep under the accumulated rubbish, until brought to light by Mr. Beglar's clearance excavations.

3 Beal's Si-yu-ki, II., 116.

figure was then buried up to the breast shows that the sand which had covered the Vajrâsan on the west side had also spread to the east.

B is the last position of the Bodhi Tree on the terrace, immediately behind the Temple, and directly over the outer Vajrâsan, V^2.

SS, silver statues of Avalokiteswara and Maitreya in two niches to the right and left of the outside door.[1] The lower part of these niches still remained intact down to the present time. The statues were 10 feet high, and were made of white silver, a fact which would have ensured their early disappearance.

W. The Walk or Promenade of Buddha. Hwen Thsang states that the place where Buddha walked up and down was to the North of the Bodhi Tree.[2] "When " Tathâgata had obtained enlightenment, he did not rise from the Throne, but remained " perfectly quiet for seven days, lost in contemplation. Then rising, he walked up and " down during seven days to the north of the Tree; he walked there east and west for a " distance of ten paces or so. Miraculous flowers sprang up under his foot traces to the " number of eighteen. Afterwards this space was covered in by a brick wall about " three feet high." I have already noticed that the 18 steps noted by Hwen Thsang show that the length of the walk must have been 20 paces, or 50 feet, instead of the 10 paces or 25 feet of his text. The Walk still exists as shown in the Map of the monuments in the courtyard, Plate XVIII. *See also* Plate XI.

U. " On the left side of the road, to the north of the place where Buddha walked, " is a large stone, on the top of which, as it stands in a great Vihâra, is a figure of " Buddha with his eyes raised, and looking up. Here in former times Buddha sat for " seven days contemplating the Bodhi Tree. He did not remove his gaze from it during " this period."[3] This building was known as the Vihâra of "Uplifted Eyes," or "Stedfast Gaze" the *Animisha-lochanam*, or "Unwinking Eyes." Its position is marked by the letter U on a large basement which goes down to the same level as the original Temple.

F is the basement of a very large Temple of early date. This corresponds with the site of a very large Vihâra to the west of the Bodhi Tree, which contained a brass figure of Buddha standing with his face to the east and adorned with jewels. Before it there was "a blue stone, with wonderful marks upon it, and strangely figured." This stone I believe to be still in existence in the Temple of Vâgeswari Devi, to the east of the Great Temple. A sketch of it has been given by Dr. Rajendra Lâl.[4] Here Buddha sat on a seven-gemmed throne made by Indra, when Brahmâ built a hall for him of seven precious substances, after he had obtained complete enlightenment.[5] From the mention of these gods I believe this to be the *Ratnaghara Chaitya*, or Palace made by the Devas (Indra and Brahmâ) where Buddha sat for seven days, and saw the whole course of his future career. The place where the Dharma was thus perceived was called *Ratnaghara Chaitya*.[6]

---

1 Beal's Si-yu-ki, II., 119.

2 Beal's Si-yu-ki, II., 122.

3 Beal's Si-yu-ki, II., 123.

4 *See* Buddha Gaya Plate, Pl. XLIII., fig. 4.

5 Beal's Si-yu-ki, II., 123.

6 Hardy, Manual of Buddhism, p. 181, makes the bearing from the Bodhi Tree N.W.; but the Chinese pilgrim is more likely to have been correct, as he actually visited the place, and described all the monuments in detail.

Fa Hian also mentions the Jewelled Chamber where the Devas worshipped Buddha for seven days. Hwen Thsang adds "from the time of the Holy One till the present is so "long that the gems have changed into stone.[1]

G is the square base or plinth of a very large stûpa of a very early period. From its position immediately to the south of the Bodhi Tree there can be no doubt that it represents the "Stûpa, 100 feet in height," which Asoka built on the spot where Buddha sat down on the bundle of *Grass*, which he received from Sakra, disguised as a grass cutter, when on his way from bathing in the Nairanjan River to the Bodhi Tree.

P represents the site of the remains of a small Stûpa to the north-east of the last, and seems to correspond in position with the Stûpa that was built on the spot where the blue *Pigeons* circled round Buddha. From its low position it must have been of an early date.

D, D. "To the east of the Bodhi Tree, on the left and right of the great road," there were two Stûpas, which marked the spot where Mâra and his daughter tempted Buddha.[2] The two small Stûpas marked D, D, completely fulfil Hwen Thsang's description, as they stand due east of the Bodhi Tree, one on each side of the road. Mâra himself and all his legions were discomfited, and his blooming daughters were changed into decrepit old women.

K. To the north-west of the Bodhi Tree, in a Vihâra, there was an image of *Kâsyapa* Buddha, which was noted for its miraculous powers. The remains of the small Vihâr, marked K, answer exactly to the described position.

E, E. To the north-west of Kâsyapa's statue there were two brick chambers, each containing the figure of an *Earth* Spirit. These were set up in remembrance of the two Spirits of the Earth, who became witnesses for Buddha, when Mâra tempted him for the last time. The site is under a high mound, on which the Burmese Rest-house now stands.

S. To the north-west of *the wall* of the Bodhi Tree, that is outside the enclosure, there was a Stûpa called *Kunkuma*, about 40 feet high. The site is now under a high mound. The Stûpa was built by a merchant of Tsaukuta, or Arachosia. The Stûpa is said to have been covered with saffron plaster, hence its name.

N, L. This site shows the remains of a Temple built upon a ruined Stûpa, with a small Stûpa in front of it. It corresponds with the spot, near the south-east angle of the Bodhi enclosure, were there was a Stûpa under a *Nyagrodha* Tree, with a Vihâra beside it, in which there was a sitting figure of Buddha. Here Brahma exhorted Buddha when he had just acquired enlightenment, to turn the wheel of the Law. A copper plate inscribed with the Buddhist creed was found here.

C^1, C^2, C^3, C^4. These four Stûpas seem to represent those which stood in the four corners of the Bodhi enclosure. After Buddha accepted the Grass (G.) he walked to all the four sides of the Bodhi Tree, while the earth trembled. On reaching the Vajrâsan the earth was still. C^4 is still nearly complete.

---

1 Giles's Fa Hian, p. 76.

2 Beal's Si-yu-ki, I., 124.

H is the ruin of a fine Temple which contained the pedestal of a statue dedicated by Mahânâma, whom I take to be the same as the author of the Mahâwanso. Here also was found a long inscription of Mahânâma. These inscriptions are described further on.

I¹, I². Two Stûpas built by Indra and Brahma, near the Stûpa where Mâra tried to frighten Buddha. The occasion on which they were built is not stated.

J. A curious Stûpa Temple, which yielded a copper coin of Raja Pasupati.

M¹. By the side of the eastern wall of the Temple there was a Stûpa marking the spot where Mâra tried to frighten Buddha.[1] The building marked M¹ is the remains of a Temple; but it stands upon an old Stûpa basement, as proved by the row of dentils just below the cornice, which goes completely round. If not, I would propose the small Stûpa marked M² a little to the north of the other just outside the eastern wall of the enclosure.

The milkmaids Stûpa is described as being outside the walls to the south-west of the Bodhi Tree. This was the site of the house of the two milkmaids who offered rice milk to Buddha. Mr. Beal calls them "*shepherd girls*," but Hindus do not make use of ewes milk. Julien more correctly calls them "deux bouvieres." By the side of the "house-Stûpa" there was a second Stûpa, where the girls boiled the rice. The site of these two Stûpas is now covered up by the great mound of rubbish which lies between the Temple court and the Budtokar Tank, due south from the Temple. *See* the Map in Plate I.

R shows the site of an old Temple of the Gupta period, which was discovered during Major Meade's excavations in 1862. It contained an inscribed statue of the later Gupta period, which was said to have been carried off by the Burmese, but which still exists at Sherghâti, at Major Meade's old house. The inscription has been published by Dr. Rajendra Lal, who has given a translation of it. A revised translation, made by Pandit Bhagwân Lal, will be found along with all the other inscriptions. *See* Plate XXVII.

T marks the spot where a colossal sitting figure of Buddha was found, near the remains of a small old Temple, with its doorway facing the north towards the Bodhi Tree. The statue is of the early Gupta style of art, with a round, plump face and a full under-lip. It bears an inscription, dated in the Samvat year 64 of Maharaja Tukamâla (or Turamâla), and is worded in the simple form of the Indo-Scythian records. *See* Plate XXV.

V¹ represents the site of the original Vajrâsan Throne inside Asoka's Temple.

V² represents the site of the outer Vajrâsan Throne, with an inscription of the Indo-Scythian period. It was immediately under the last position of the Bodhi Tree.

X shows the spot where the copper gilt umbrella of Dharma Raja Guru was found, buried 8 feet below the level of the modern surface of the Burmese clearings. The inscription is dated in the Burmese Saka Raj year, 397, or A.D. 1035. *See* Plates XVIII and XXIX.

---

[1] Beal's Si-yu-ki, II., 132.

Y is an octagonal well on the south or right hand side of the road immediately outside the eastern gate of the present enclosure. It is worthy of notice that most of the old Buddhist wells are octagonal.

Z^1 shows the spot where the two small Chinese inscriptions were found.

Z^2 shows the spot where the two large Chinese inscriptions were found, one of them broken. They were probably brought from the Stûpas, marked Z^3 in the plan, as this spot corresponds exactly with the distance of 30 paces, or 75 feet, to the north of the Bodhidrûma, where the pilgrim Yun-shu states that he erected a stone Stûpa in honour of the ten thousand Buddhas. *See* No. 1 Chinese inscription.

Z^4 marks the spot where the Chinese inscription with the eight figures was found. *See* No. 5 Chinese inscription.

XI.—MONUMENTS OUTSIDE THE WALLS.

The following monuments were all outside the walls. They are described by Hwen Thsang alone. *See* Beal's Si-yu-ki, II., 127 to 133, and Julien's Hwen Thsang II., 477. All the letters refer to the map in Plate I.

To the south of the Bodhi Tree, outside the walls, for about 10 *li*, or 1½ mile, the sacred monuments were so numerous that Hwen Thsang found it difficult to describe them. At the present day there are few traces of buildings more than half a mile distant on any side, but within this range there still remain several fine tanks. All of these tanks are surrounded by earthen mounds, in which are probably concealed the remains of many of the monuments described by the pilgrim. The identification of some of the principal places is certain, while that of several others is only doubtful as to which side of one of the known positions it ought to be looked for. I will now describe these in the same order as they are noted by Hwen Thsang, using again the letters of the alphabet for reference to the map in Plate I.

A. Outside the south gate of the Bodhi Tree enclosure there was a great tank, about 700 paces, or 1,750 feet, in circuit. "This was the pond that was dug by the two "Brahman brothers." This is beyond all doubt the fine tank 400 feet due south of the Great Temple, which is now called *Buddhokar* or *Buddha Pokhar*, that is, "Buddha's Tank." It still retains the same dimensions as in the time of Hwen Thsang. Its northern bank is permanently defined by a long wall with ornamented niches, and steps leading down to the water.

B. Still further to the south there was another tank which was made by Indra, when Buddha, after he had attained perfect intelligence, formed a wish to bathe. This may be identified with the tank of *Ghosal Chak*, or "bathing tank," as it is now called, which lies 300 feet to the south-west of the Buddhokar, but is to the south-west of the Great Temple.

C. To the west of this tank there was a large stone, which Indra brought from the Snowy Mountains, when Buddha wished to dry his clothes after bathing. No stone is there now, nor is there any trace beside it of the Stûpa D, where Buddha put on the clothes given him by a poor old woman, nor of the Stûpa, E, where he received the clothes from the woman.

F. To the east of the tank created by Indra for Buddha to bathe in, and in the midst of a wood, was the tank of Muchilinda, King of the Nâgas. On its west bank there was a small Vihâra G, containing a figure of Buddha. The easterly bearing points to the tank on the south-east of the village of Urel, or Uruvilwa, on the west bank of which, across a small stream, must have stood the small Vihâr containing a figure of Buddha. The house of the blind Nâga is placed by Hwen Thsang outside the eastern gate of the wall of the Bodhi Tree, at a distance of 2 or 3 *li*, or nearly half a mile. It must therefore have been on the bank of the river behind the Mahant's courtyard. The Nâga recovered his sight as Buddha passed by on his way to the Bodhi Tree.

H. To the east of Muchilinda's tank there was a Vihâra in a wood, which contained a figure of Buddha, representing him as thin and withered away. This site may be fixed on a small mound to the south of the village of Urel, and to the east of the Muchilinda (or Urel) tank.

J. Beside it there was a long promenade of 70 paces, where Buddha walked up and down for exercise. On each side of it there was a Pipal Tree.

K. Beside the Pipal Tree, where Buddha had fasted, there was a Stûpa, where Ajnâta Kaundinya and his four companions had lived.

L. To the *south-west* of this spot there was a Stûpa marking the spot where Buddha entered the Nairanjan River to bathe. The mention of the river shows conclusively that the bearing should be south-*east*. This spot may be fixed at Tika Bigha, near the river.

M. Close by, on the bank of the river, was the place where Buddha received the rice-milk. At this spot there are some masonry remains, buried deep, on the very edge of the river; part has been carried away by the stream.

N. Near the last was the place where the merchants offered Buddha wheat, flour, and honey. As the merchants were travelling along the road, the site of Tika Bigha, fixed for the place where Buddha entered the river to bathe, is most probably correct.

P. Beside the last place was the spot where the four kings (of the four quarters of the world) each offered a golden bowl to Buddha, in which to place the flour and honey given by the merchants. Buddha sat silent, and did not accept the golden bowls. The four kings then offered silver bowls, and afterwards vessels of crystal, lapis lazuli, cornelian, amber, ruby, and so on. But Buddha would not accept any of them. They then brought stone pâtras, which Buddha, having joined into one vessel, accepted, so as to avoid receiving one and refusing the others. "Putting them one within the other, he " made made one vessel of the four, showing four distinct borders on the outside of " the rim."

R. At a short distance from the last spot there was a Stûpa, where Tathâgata preached the law for the sake of his mother, who had come down from the heavens to hear him.

S. Close by there was a dry pool and a Stûpa, where Buddha had displayed various spiritual changes.

U. Beside the last was the spot where Buddha converted Uruvilwa Kâsyapa and his two brothers, with a thousand of their followers.

These last three sites, R, S, U, Mr. Beglar thinks should be placed about one-third of a mile to the south of M, where some masonry remains still exist. I think that Mr. Beglar must be right, as Hwen Thsang states that the sacred traces extend for 10 *li* or 1⅔ mile to the south of Bodhi Tree.

V. To the north-west of the last place there was a Stûpa to mark the spot where Buddha subdued the fiery Nâga, to which Uruvilwa Kâsyapa sacrificed. This subject is often represented in Buddhist sculptures.

W. By the side of this last there was another Stûpa, where 500 Pratyeka Buddhas entered Niwâna at the same time.

X. To the south of the Muchilinda tank there was a Stûpa marking the spot where Kâsyapa went to save Buddha during an inundation.

XII.—MONASTERY OF MAHÂBODHI-SANGHÂRÂMA.

The building next in importance to the Great Temple was the Mahâbodhi Sanghârâma, or Monastery of the Bodhi Tree. The earliest mention of it is by Fa Hian in A.D. 409, who says, "at the place where Buddha attained perfect wisdom there are *three* "monasteries, all inhabited by priests. The priests and people gave (the pilgrims) what "food they required without stint.[1]" The mention of the number of *three* monasteries is important, as Hwen Thsang says that this monastery had *six* halls, by which I understand *six* distinct buildings.[2] It had pavilions three stories high, and was surrounded by a wall from 30 to 40 feet in height. It was richly ornamented in red and blue colours, and possessed lofty Stûpas containing relics of Buddha. It contained also a statue of Buddha, cast in gold and silver, and decorated with gems and precious stones. The relics were publicly exhibited every year at the full moon [or 30th day of the 12th month, according to Mr. Beal], that is, on the last day of Chaitra, immediately preceding the first of Vaisâkh badi. The priests were upwards of 1,000 in number.

Hwen Thsang attributes the building of the monastery to a king of Ceylon.[3] "In "old days," he says, "there was a king of Ceylon, which is a country of the Southern "Sea, who was truthful, and a believer in the law of Buddha. It happened that his "brother, who had become a disciple of Buddha, thinking on the holy traces of Buddha, "went forth to wander through India. At all the convents he visited he was treated "with disdain as a foreigner." He therefore returned to Ceylon, and induced the king "to build convents throughout all India." Being furnished with money, he returned to India, where he was informed that "the Bôdhi is the place where all the past Buddhas "have obtained the holy fruit, and where the future ones will obtain it. There is no "better place than this for carrying out the project." He accordingly built a monastery at Mahâbodhi, and set up the following inscription, engraved on copper. "To help all "without distinction is the highest teaching of all the Buddhas; to exercise mercy as "occasion offers is the illustrious doctrine of former saints. And now I, unworthy "descendant in the royal line, have undertaken to found this Sanghârâma, to enclose "the sacred traces, and to hand down their renoun to future ages, and to spread their "benefits among the people. The priests of my country will thus obtain independence,

---

1 Giles, p. 77.

2 Beal's Si-yu-ki, II., 133.

3 Beal's Si-yu-ki, II., 133.

" and be treated as members of the fraternity of this country. Let this privilege be " handed down from generation to generation without interruption."

I have quoted this inscription at length chiefly because the writer declares himself to be of the royal family of Ceylon. As Mahânâma does the same in the inscription which he set up in a temple near the Bodhi Tree, I cannot help thinking that he must have been the agent of the King of Ceylon, who was employed to build the monastery. If I am right in supposing that Hwen Thsang's *six* halls mean six distinct monasteries, then it is evident that *three* of them must have been built some time after Fa Hian's visit, when their number was only *three*. Now, Mahânâma, the Buddhist Priest, and author of the Mahâwanso, was a member of the Royal Family of Ceylon, as he specially states in his Mahâbodhi inscription,[1] and, as he visited Mahâbodhi some time after Fa Hian, there is no chronological difficulty to prevent the acceptance of my suggestion, that he was very probably the relative of the king of Ceylon who superintended the building of the Mahâbodhi Monastery.

The Vajrâsan Mahâbodhi Monastery is mentioned again, about A.D. 670, by the pilgrim Hwuï Lun, as " the same as the one built by a king of Ceylon, in which priests " of that country formerly dwelt."

The position of the Great Monastery to the north of the Great Temple corresponds exactly with the extensive mound known as Amar Sinh's Fort. The lofty walls of the monastery, from 30 to 40 feet in height, would naturally have led to its occupation as a fort *after the decline of Buddhism*, in the 11th century. The date of Amar Sinh in quite uncertain; but as he is said to have been a *Suïr*, or aboriginal *Savara*, I conclude that he must have held power before the rise of the Pâla Rajas, in 800 A.D. Buchanan mentions that the mound was called Râjasthân, or " the Palace," a name which is now confined to the group of buildings outside the north-west corner of the monastery enclosure. Other buildings at the north-east corner are also called Rânivâs, or the " Râni's Palace." Perhaps these names may refer to the period of Amar Sinh's rule.

The mound is from 1,500 to 2,000 feet in length from west to east, and nearly 1,000 feet in breadth from north to south. The land of the mound still retains the general name of *Mahâbodhi*. Here, in November 1885, Mr. Beglar and myself discovered the remains of a great monastery, with outer walls 9 feet thick, and massive round towers at the four corners. The enclosure which surrounded the monastery had already been traced by Mr. Beglar, at a distance of about 100 feet all round. One tower of this enclosure is still standing on the west side in an old Muhammadan burial ground, and the outer line of wall with the south-west tower are still traceable. There were four towers at the four corners, and three intermediate towers on each side, making a total of 16 towers.

The plan of the monastery is laid out after the usual Hindu fashion in a diagram of squares, *see* Plate XX. The plan consists of 36 squares, six on each side, of which the four corner squares are assigned to the corner towers, and the four middle squares to an open pillared court containing a well. Each square is 26 feet 6 inches side, or 18 cubits of 17·66 inches, or 16 cubits of nearly 20 inches each.

[1] In Mr. Fleet's Corpus Inscript. Ind., No. 71, line 20, he calls himself *Langka-dwipaprasutah*.

The centre of the court lies due north from the pinnacle of the Great Temple, but the east and west line of the monastery bears 96° 30′, or 6° 30′ south of east, that is, just half a Nakshatra space, or $360° \div 27 \div 2 = 6° 40'$, an amount of deviation which I have found in most ancient buildings, but more especially in those of the Gupta period.

A long covered drain leads from the well to the outside of the walls on the north-north-west, ending in a gargoyle spout in the shape of a large crocodile's head, of dark blue basalt, richly carved.

The main body of the monastery occupies the 16 interior squares, with the four outer walls placed outside. This square is $26' 6'' \times 4 = 106$ feet. In the middle of the east and west sides there is an extension equal to two squares, each extension forming one large room. On the north and south sides there is a small extension, each forming a single small room, which, apparently, was only accessible from the inside.

The open courtyard in the middle was surrounded by a cloister supported on pillars, of which several bases were found *in situ*. On all four sides of the cloister there were small groups of cells, arranged as shown in the plan. On the north and south sides the centre cells led into the small rooms, which were outside the main line of wall. These inner rooms probably contained statues of Buddha, but the other rooms were, no doubt, the cells or dwelling-rooms of the superior monks. Only one statue, of gold and silver, is mentioned by Hwen Thsang, and this probably occupied the outer cell on the north side, with the middle cell as a hall in front of it. The outer cell on the south side may have been the Treasury and Relic Chamber of the monastery. The remaining chambers on the ground floor could not have accommodated more than 16 monks. A second storey might have held 20 more, and if there had been a third storey the whole number of cells would not have held more than 56 monks. I conclude, therefore, that the lower orders of priests must have been lodged in chambers arranged inside the walls of the surrounding enclosure, which was about 400 feet square. As the wall of this enclosure is said by Hwen Thsang to have been from 30 to 40 feet in height, there may have been three storeys of chambers; and, as each side of the enclosure was about 400 feet in length, the whole length of the rows of chambers would have been from 1,500 to 1,600 feet in each storey, equal to about 600 apartments. But, as the number of monks is said by Hwen Thsang to have been about 1,000, I conclude that there must have been other smaller monasteries on the great mound, the sites of which still remain to be discovered.

I conjecture that the four towers or pavilions at the corners of the monastery, which were three storeys in height, must have had domed roofs terminating in *âmalaka* pinnacles.

I believe also that there must have been a large Stûpa in the middle of the open court of the monastery. Hwen Thsang mentions large Stûpas which contained relics of Buddha. These must have been outside the walls of the central building, but within the great enclosure.

The outer walls of the monastery were 9 feet thick. The plinth on which they rested was 7 feet 9 inches high, with a series of mouldings projecting 13½ inches on the outside, and two offsets on the inside projecting 3 inches, as shown in Plate XXI.

The floor of the monastery was level with the top of the plinth, and that of the courtyard outside was 5 feet 9 inches lower, or just 2 feet above the foot of the plinth. The courtyard of the enclosure was nearly 20 feet above the level of the courtyard of the Great Temple, and the floor of the monastery was just 25 feet above that level, or almost exactly on the same level as the top of the basement of the Temple.

The great flight of steps leading from the Temple to the monastery, with the lower part of the surrounding wall, are shown in Plate XXI.

XIII.—VOTIVE STÛPAS.

When Buddhist pilgrims visited any of the famous sites connected with the history of their great teacher it was their invariable custom to make some offering, no matter how small or poor, to the shrine, and at the same time to set up some memorial of their visit. The offerings consisted of money and precious stones, vessels and costly cloths by the rich, and of fruits and flowers by the poor. The memorials generally took the form of temples and large Stûpas by the wealthy, and of small Stûpas, or inscribed slabs by the poor. In Burma, where Buddhism still flourishes, these memorials are very numerous; and the courtyards of the great Stûpas at Rangoon and Prome, both of which I have seen, are so crowded with them that they actually touch one another. Such also was the case at Mahâbodhi, as described by Hwen Thsang, who says, "Within "the surrounding wall the sacred traces touch one another in all directions. Here "there are *Stûpas*, in another place *Vihâras*. The kings, princes, and great personages " . . have erected these monuments as memorials."[1]

In my account of the inscriptions I have described the memorial Vihâra, erected by the Ceylonese pilgrim Mahânâma, in the middle of the 5th century A.D., as well as the Stûpas set up by Chinese pilgrims in the 11th century. But these are only specimens of the hundreds of monuments which still remain to attest the religious enthusiasm of the Buddist votaries. The almost countless numbers of these monuments may be best realised by a glance at the map in Plate XVIII., and at the views of the courtyard in Plate XIX., which shows only the lower stratum of the earlier Stûpas and Vihâras that still remain, about 200 in number. Above these were some four tiers of similar monuments in a still more ruinous condition from their exposure to the ravages of the villagers. But all these are only the structural Stûpas which were built up of separate stones and bricks. By far the greatest number of the monuments consisted of *thousands* of monolith Stûpas of all sizes, from 2 feet in diameter down to 2 inches. Five specimens of various heights are given in Plate XXIII., A to E.[2] The same countless multitude of small Stûpas was found by Kittoe and myself around the great Stûpa of Dhamek, at Sârnâth, Benares. But there were hundreds of thousands of even smaller offerings in the shape of little clay Stûpas, both baked and unbaked, from 2 or 3 inches in height, to the size of a walnut. Scores, and sometimes even hundreds, of these

---

[1] Beal's Si-yu-ki, II. 215.

[2] Three specimens of early Stûpas are given in F, G, and H of the same Plate, from the bas-reliefs. J and K are structural Stûpas of stone.

miniature Stûpas were found inside the larger Stûpas, enclosing small clay seals. I have made similar finds at other places, and these small Stûpas would appear to have been the common form of memorial for the poorer pilgrims.

There is a great variety in the shapes of these votive Stûpas, from the low and almost bare hemisphere of the time of Asoka to the tall ornamented spire surmounting the mediæval dome, with its elaborately carved basement. One example shown in Plate XIX., in middle of front row, was exhumed absolutely intact; its pinnacle was afterwards removed or stolen. In the accompanying Plate XXIII. I have given specimens of the Stûpas of different ages, beginning with the rude rough monoliths of the early periods, all of which are of granite and without ornament of any kind.[1] Richly ornamented specimens of the same forms are found amongst the bas-reliefs of Bharhut and Sânchi, but those sculptured on the still earlier Railing of Mahâbodhi are without decoration.

The earliest Stûpas would appear to have been simple barrows or mounds of earth. After a time the earthen mounds were faced with brick or stone, as at Srâvasti; and still later they were built throughout of stones in a hilly country, as at Sânchi and Bharhut, and of bricks in the plain country, as at Ahichatra and Srâvasti. The earliest Stûpas are simple hemispheres raised on a single low basement, about half the diameter in height, as at Manikyâla, Sânchi, and other places near Bhilsa. Gradually the plinth was increased in height, until, in the time of the Indo-Scythians, it rose from one to two diameters in height, of which the finest existing example is the great Stûpa of Dhamek at Sârnâth Benares, which was built about the 6th century A.D.

All of these old Stûpas would appear to have been crowned by umbrellas, either of stone or of gilt copper, as represented in the bas-reliefs at Mahâbodhi, Bharhut, and Sânchi, as well as in the rock cut Stûpas in the caves of Dhamnâr and Kholvi in Central India. The same style still exists in Burma, where all the great Stûpas are crowned by a succession of umbrellas one over the other, gradually diminishing in size.

At a later date, during the reign of the Pâla kings in Magadha, the style of these votive Stûpas was much altered, the basement being still further heightened, and the number of umbrellas increased to 9 and 11, and even to 13, with a vase full of fruits forming a finial on the top. The whole height of the Stûpa thus became equal to three or four diameters of the hemisphere. At the same time figures of Buddha were placed in niches on each side of the square base, while the different tiers of mouldings were separated by rows of sculptured figures. These generally consisted of lines of small niches filled with figures of Buddha, or of rows of small Stûpas. In some cases the donor himself is represented below, with his gifts arranged on each side of him.

I have given two of these tall mediæval Stûpas. Both of them have lost their finials, but I have supplied two, A and B, from well-preserved examples found in the ruins.

J and K show the common form of octagonal Stûpa, with four projecting faces containing figures of Buddha in niches, and a single tier of base mouldings, also decorated with figures.

---

[1] *See* Plate VII., South Railing, inner face, second pillar from left, uppermost medallion.

Other examples are much larger, with figures and ornamented mouldings between the four projecting faces.

One has a single projecting face, which is hollowed out to form a chamber, like a small Temple, for the reception of a figure of Buddha.

In all the later examples of the votive Stûpa the lines of moulding are more numerous and much more elaborate.

In these late examples the dome, which was originally the principal feature of the Stûpa, becomes a mere finish or top to a series of elaborate lines of decorated mouldings forming a lofty base. Two examples of this kind are shown in figures J and K of Plate XXIII.

Above the dome, the single umbrella, or the few tiers of three or five umbrellas, became a tall spire of from 9 to 13 successive tiers of umbrellas; surmounted by a small vessel containing fruit or flowers rising like a cone or flame to a point. In Plate XXIII. I have given one example of these finials from specimens found amongst the ruins. This largest one, C, which is 5½ inches in diameter, must have belonged to a Stûpa at least double the size of those shown in the Plate, or about 10 to 12 feet in height.

I take this vase finial to be the exact representation of the pinnacle which originally crowned the great temple of Mahâbodhi. Hwen Thsang describes it as an *O-mo-lo-kia-ko* fruit, in gilt copper. M. Julien notes that a Chinese note explains the term by *Pao-ping*, "vase precieux"; and he adds that the Chinese syllables must represent *Amala-Karka*, "*vase-pur*."[1] Mr. Beal corrects this reading to *Amara-Karka*, the "immortal dish."[2] But I believe that the true rendering is *âmala-Karka*, the "*âmala vase*," or vessel in shape like an *âmala* or *Aonla* fruit. That this is the correct explanation seems to be certain from Hwen Thsang's own rendering of the term in another place, where he explains that it is the "name of a fruit used as a medicine in India."[3] Now the *âmala* or *Aonla* is a well known fruit (the Phyllanthus emblica, or emblic myrobalan), which is nearly spherical in shape, like the vase or water vessel (*Karka*) in the Plate. As the Aonla fruit is still used as a medicine in India, prepared as a preserve, the explanation of the *O-mo-lo-kia-ko* as an *âmala-Karka*, or "Aonla shaped vessel," seems to be quite clear and satisfactory.

The pinnacle of the Great Temple, as restored by the Burmese in the 11th century, did not show any traces of the *Aonla* vase, the principal feature being a very flat projecting circle with a crenated or indented edge. The fruit is also called *âmalaka*.

In the accompanying Plate XIX. it will be seen that not one of the structural Stûpas is now perfect.[4] The pinnacles of the tall mediæval Stûpas were always more or less broken, and even the solid hemispheres of the earlier structural Stûpas were mostly displaced. These last would no doubt have remained intact down to the present day, had they not been overturned by the builders of later ages. Carved stones of an early date were

---

1 Julien's Hwen Thsang, II. 464. 2 Beal's Si-yu-ki, II. 137, note. 3 Beal's Si-yu-ki, II. 95.

4 One was found quite perfect, terminating in a finial like A and B in Plate XXIII.; but it was afterwards lost or stolen.

frequently found in the bases of the later monuments, and as the soil got silted up, the general level of the courtyard was gradually raised, and the later Stûpas were built over the tops of the earlier ones in successive tiers of different ages. Thus Temples have been found standing on broken Stûpas, and Stûpas resting upon ruined Temples. So great was the number of these successive monuments, and so rapid was the accumulation of stones and earth, that the general level of the courtyard was raised abcut 20 feet above the floor of the Great Temple.

XIV.—SEALS WITH FIGURES AND INSCRIPTIONS.

Buddhist seals are found in very great numbers at every Buddhist site, and in small numbers at every old city. By far the greater number are of clay, both burnt and unburnt, but I have several in metal and a few in ivory. According to the rules laid down in the Buddhist scriptures, the monks might have seals of copper, brass, bell-metal, ivory, or horn, but not of gold, silver, or precious stones. The subject engraved on the seal was limited to a "circle, with two deer on opposite sides, and below them the name "of the founder of the Vihâr." A layman might have "either a full-length human figure "or a head cut on his seal."[1] Of the monks' seals I have seen a few specimens, of which I have published one found in the ruins at Sârnâth. Above are two antelopes facing each other, and below a short inscription of two lines opening with *Sri Saddharmma* in the upper line, and naming *Gandha-kuti* in the second line as the Temple to which the owner was attached.[2]

Of the laymen's seals there are no doubt many examples; but unless the subjects or the names are distinctly Buddhist, it is difficult to distinguish mere heads and figures with common names from Brahmanical seals. I have published one seal which most probably belongs to this class.[3] It is a sardonyx, and bears a pair of feet above a throne, with a worshipper on each side. Below there is an inscription of four letters, which I cannot read satisfactorily. A few other seals found in the excavations at Mahâhodhi may be accepted as being most probably Buddhist from their Buddhist findspot.

In Plate XXIV. I have inserted four seals of this kind. Fig. 1, of grey clay, bears the following inscription, in characters of the 1st or 2nd century B.C.:—"*Mokhali* "*kasa*," the last letter only being doubtful. The name seems to have reference to the powerful tribe of the *Maukharis*, if so, this is by far the earliest record which has been found of them.

Fig. 2 is a round impression in black clay, with a half lotus flower above the name of *Kumâra*. The characters belong to the 5th or 6th century A.D.

Fig. 3 is a round impression in clay of a mediæval seal bearing the name of *Râjni Sri Soma-Tula*.

Fig. 4 is an oblong seal impression of black clay, bearing the name of "*Kasaparakshita*" in mediæval letters, for Kâsyapa-Rakshita.

[1] Csoma de Köros, in Asiatic Researches, XX. 86.
[2] Archæological Survey, Vol. I., Plate XXXIV.
[3] Archæological Survey, Vol. I., Plate VII.

In Plate XXIV. I have collected together sketches of all the principal seals found at Mahâ-badhi, both before and during the excavations. All of them, excepting the four just described, I take to be monastic seals of mediæval date. Figures A and D were obtained some years before the excavations were begun, along with several others, all of which were more or less broken. The others were found during the excavations, chiefly in ruined Stûpas and Temples, and are consequently in very fine preservation. All of them are of burnt clay, mostly red, but some are greyish yellow, and a few are quite black. They are all represented of half size. The originals are now in the British Museum.

A is a broken terra-cotta figure of Padmapâṇi, with the seal of the monastery stamped near the right shoulder. It contains nothing besides the well-known Buddhist creed.

B—only a few examples of this seal have been found, all in good order. Its arrangement is altogether exceptional. Buddha is represented seated with both hands in his lap, inside a pillared temple with a low roof. There is no inscription or other indication of its age, but from its appearance I judge that it is not older than the 10th or 11th century.

C is also an exceptional seal, as Buddha is represented seated on a throne with his hands raised before his breast in the attitude of teaching. The seal was probably brought by a pilgrim from Benares.

On all the remaining large seals in D, E, F, Buddha is represented in the well-known attitude which he assumed when seated under the Bodhi Tree in meditation. These, therefore, are the proper seals of the different Buddhist establishments at Mahâbodhi. Most of them are in excellent preservation, the edges being crisp and unbroken. The inscriptions consist of the well-known Buddhist creed in mediæval characters.

It is necessary to remark that the attitude of Buddha as represented on these seals, as well as in all the mediæval statues and bas-reliefs, agrees exactly with that described by Hwen Thsang as the posture of the statue of Buddha in the great Temple, when he visited it in A.D. 635. He says, "In the vihâra they found a beautiful figure of Buddha "in a sitting position, the right foot uppermost, the left hand resting, the right hand "hanging down." I may add that the left hand rests in the lap with the palm uppermost, while the palm of the right hand rests on the right knee, showing the back of the hand to the spectator. This is the precise attitude of the original Vajrâsan Buddha in the central niche at the back of the Temple. The right hand points to the earth as his witness.

The smaller seals represented in the Plate, 5, 6, 7, with the four exceptions already referred to as belonging to laymen, are all monastic seals with long inscriptions, which are very difficult to read. A Stûpa is the only type of most of them, sometimes occupying the whole field, as on fig. 5, or placed below, as on figs. 6, 9, 22, or in the middle of the inscription, as on figs. 7, 8, and 12. With two exceptions, figs. 15 and 16, which are of crude clay, they are all of burnt clay. I do not expect that they will yield any valuable information, as they most probably contain in addition to the well-known creed only a few religious formulæ, as in the last line of fig. 6, which reads "*Visuddha-swâhâ.*"

All the seals in Plate XXIV. were found in the ruined Stûpas and Temples during the excavations. It was the custom, however, to stamp the larger clay figures of Buddha with seals containing the Buddhist creed, of which a fine example has been deposited in the British Museum. This image was found in one of the niches on the east face of the Temple very near the top. The representation is one half the size of the original. Its preservation is almost wonderful when we remember that it must have been exposed for upwards of eight centuries to the heavy rains of Bengal.

Thousands of small seals of crude unburnt clay were also found in the Stûpas along with numbers of cowree shells, and in one instance a small copper coin of Pasupati, Raja of Nepal.[1] In four instances small flat copper plates were found with the Buddhist creed engraved upon them, the oldest being about the 9th or 10th century, and the others of the 11th century. Two of these are shown in the accompanying Plate XXVII., figs. F and K. Of these fig. F appears to be the oldest.

The remaining Stûpa seals are not shown in the Plates. Fig. 5 is a single specimen of these seals. It is made of an extremely fine hard clay of a grey colour, which has taken and preserved a very sharp impression. The inscription has not been read.

Fig. 6 has an inscription of 14 lines above a small Stûpa. This will probably be deciphered, as there are numerous examples for comparison.

Fig. 7, which is more than 2 inches long, has an inscription of 19 lines of small letters, with a small Stûpa in the middle. It is fairly legible, and I have succeeded in reading several portions of it. In the 10th and 14th lines I find the word *pratishthita*—"established."

Figs. 8 to 12 are similar seals, but rather smaller, and figs. 13 and 14 are examples of the commonest kind of unbaked clay seals with the usual creed.

Of figs. 15 and 16 only a few crude specimens were found in an injured state, as they had evidently been shut up before they were dry. Both are inscribed.

In one case a model Stûpa of iron filled with clay, and containing an unbaked creed seal, was found in a small ruined Stûpa. Great numbers of round and oblong balls of clay were also discovered. On being broken they were found to contain from one to three or four small unbaked seals. Similar balls have been dug up at most Buddhist sites. Numerous miniature Stûpas were also found in baked clay, each of which was found to contain a small seal with the Buddhist creed.

---

[1] Plate XXVII., fig. H.

XV.—SCULPTURES.

The early Buddhists had no statues of Buddha. He is not once represented in the sculptured bas-reliefs of Bharhut, which date from 150 to 100 B.C., and there is no image of him amongst the numerous scenes of the great Sânchi Stûpa. The oldest representations of Buddha, that I am aware of, are found on the coins of the Indo-Scythian king, Kanishka, about A.D. 100. But the art of sculpture was certainly known and practised by the Hindus as early as the time of Asoka, as the old Buddhist Railing of the Mahâbodhi Temple, with its inscriptions in Asoka characters, is not only ornamented with numerous sculptured medallions, but also with a full length figure of a Yakshini climbing a tree, with her right foot supported by a seated Yaksha below. The single remaining pillar of the canopy of Buddha's walk also bears a full length female figure of half life size, and as both the shaft and the base of this pillar were marked with the Asoka letter A, whilst other bases are marked with other Asoka characters, there can be no doubt that this sculpture must belong to the 3rd century B.C.

I think also that the Vajrâsan slab, ornamented with a geometrical pattern on top, which was found outside the Great Temple under the shadow of the Bodhi Tree, must belong to the same age, as the geese and parrots, with other conventional ornaments, are exactly similar in style and treatment with those which are found on the capitals of the undoubted Asoka pillars.

But the earliest figure of Buddha which has yet been found at Mahâbodhi is most probably coeval with the building of the Great Temple, about the middle of the 2nd century A.D. This statue has the full lips and round face of the Gupta style, which are seen in all the Gupta sculptures from Sârnâth, and in the single figure at Deoriya, which was carved during the reign of Kumâra Gupta. The Mahâbodhi statue bears an inscription of Mahârâja *Tukamâla* or *Turamâla* dated in the Samvat year 64, which, if referred to the Seleukidan era, would give the year 152 A.D., in the middle of the reign of the Indo-Scythian king, Huvishka.[1] It is, therefore, of about the same age as the Indo-Grecian sculptures of Gândhâra. The figure is a seated colossus, 3 feet 9 inches high, including its inscribed pedestal, by 3 feet 1 inch in breadth across the knees, which would represent a standing statue about 7 feet in height.

Amongst the Mathura sculptures there are many representations of Buddha, most of which belong to the 2nd century A.D., during the reigns of the Indo-Scythian

[1] This date is obtained by accepting the year 64 as representing 464 with the figures for hundreds omitted, as 464—312 B.C.=152 A.D. *See* Plate XXV. If referred to the Saka Samvat of A.D. 78, the date will be 10 years earlier, or A.D. 142.

princes Kanishka, Huvishka, and Vâsu Deva, whose inscriptions are found on the pedestals of the sculptures. Several of the Mathura statues of Buddha are of colossal size, ranging from 9 to 12 feet in height. It is worthy of note that the stone of which this statue is made is a sandstone like that of Mathura, and not from a local quarry. The nearest sandstone of this kind occurs near Sahsarâm to the west of the Son River.

At Mahâbodhi by far the greatest number of the figures of Buddha represent him seated under the Bodhi Tree during the six years asceticism. But the ancient examples are very few, nearly the whole mass of sculpture that now exists being of the mediæval period, during the flourishing rule of the Pâla kings, from A.D. 800 to 1200. In the time of Aṣoka sandstone was the favourite material both for architecture and sculpture. Thus the Aṣoka Railing round the Temple was chiefly if not wholly made of sandstone, so also were all the pillars of the canopied walk, as well as the Vajrâsan throne inside the Temple. Afterwards granite was commonly used for all purposes, for architecture as well as for sculptures, and for most of the votive Stûpas. Basalt, however, had already come into use for inscriptions, for which it was admirably adapted by its hardness and durability. The last facing of the Vajrâsan throne inside the Temple, which was certainly seen by Hwen Thsang in A.D. 637, was also made of blue basalt. The introduction of basalt may, therefore, be dated from about the fifth century, when it was used for the inscription of Mahânâma.

The largest figure of Buddha now existing is that which has recently been enshrined inside the Great Temple. It was formerly almost hidden inside a small room in the courtyard of the Brahmanical monastery, but it was given up by the Mahant to replace the modern brick and mud mortar statue set up by the Burmese. The figure is 5½ feet in height, which is far below the dimensions of the old statute seen by Hwen Thsang, who records that it was 11 feet 5 inches in height, with a breadth across the shoulders of 6 feet 2 inches, and across the knees of 8 feet 8 inches.[1] Its full height, if standing, would therefore have been rather more than 20 feet.

The sculptures which still exist at Buddha Gayâ and in its neighbourhood are thousands in number. The Buddhist Railing round the Temple presents some of the oldest sculptures in India, as there can be no doubt that a great part of it must have belonged to the original Temple of Asoka. This is proved by the inscriptions in Asoka characters which still exist on the Pillars, the Bars, and the Coping. The next in age is the colossal statue of Buddha, which was set up during the time of Maharaja Tukamâla, while the Indo-Scythians still held sway in Northern India. It is dated in the Samvat year 64, or, according to my calculations, A.D. 152, in the reign of the great King Huvishka. *See* Plate XXV. If referred to the Saka era, the date will be A.D. 142.

The next in age was the statue set up by the Sthâvira Mahânâma of Ceylon in the 5th century A.D. The statue itself is gone, but its inscribed pedestal still remains, together with a long inscription on a separate slab. *See* Fleet's Inscriptions of the Early Gupta Kings, pp. 274–278. The pedestal was found *in situ* in the Temple erected by Mahânâma.

For the three following centuries, from 500 to 800 A.D., the only sculpture that I can assign with any certainty is a seated figure of Buddha canopied by the Nâga king

---

[1] Beal's Si-yu-ki., II. 120.

Muchilinda. This I am induced to ascribe to about A.D. 600, from the forms of the letters in the Buddhist creed, which is inscribed on its back. The sculpture is injured, and the inscription, which I have given in Plate XXVII., fig. E, is incomplete, but the letters *y*, *th*, and *r* are certainly as old as the end of the 5th century. For comparison I have given in Plate XXVII., fig. D, a copy of the inscription on the Nirvâna statue of Buddha at Kusinagara, which was seen by Hwen Thsang in A.D. 637. I have also given for comparison a copy of the Rock Seal of Ṣaṣângka in the fort of Rohtâs, fig. G, which cannot be later than A.D. 600. With these may be compared a later inscription, fig. F, in which the letters *y* and *th* are of a later form, while the *sra* is older than the same character in the Pâla inscriptions of Plate XXVIII., which begin with A.D. 813.

The great mass of the sculptures belongs to the period of the Pâla kings, who reigned from A.D. 813 down to the Muhammadan conquest in A.D. 1201. In the sculptures of this period, of which I have seen many dated specimens, there are numberless figures of the Buddha Sâkyamuni sitting under the Bodhi Tree. This figure is generally known as the Vajrâsan Buddha. *See* Plate XXVI., No. 2. The figures of Padmapâṇi [Avalokiteswara] are also very numerous. No. 3 of Plate XXVI. is said to be a standing figure of this Bodhisatwa.

In No. 1 of Plate XXVI. I have given a photograph, full size, of the only representation of the *Tri-ratna*, the "Three-gems" or Buddhist Triad, that I have ever seen. *Buddha* is seated in the middle under the Bodhi Tree, with *Dharma* on his left hand, and *Sangha* on his right hand. Here Dharma has only two arms. The inscription seems to be as late as the 12th century.

But much of the sculpture now existing at Buddha Gaya and in its neighbourhood reveals the complete adoption of the Tântrika system of mediæval Brahmanism. The chief figure is that of Mahâkâla, or Ṣiva, whose images are still common in Nepâl, Tibet, and Ladâk. He is represented dancing on a corpse, with a bowl of blood in his left hand, a drawn sword in his upraised right hand, and a serpent round his neck. In some representations he has four arms and is clothed, but he is more often quite naked. He is in fact the God of Death, and prayers are addressed to him to avert death.

Another very common figure is the three-headed goddess *Vajra-Varâhi*, who is also known as Vasudhârâ. One of her heads is that of a pig, and there are always seven boars on the pedestal of her statue. She has eight arms, and is represented naked above the waist. She always carries a *Vajra* or thunderbolt in one hand—hence her name of *Vajra-Varâhi*, or the "Thunderbolt-Pig" goddess. I have given a good representation of this goddess in Plate XXX. from a figure which I dug up at Kurkihâr in Magadha. It is introduced here to illustrate the figures shown in the top of the Chinese Inscription No. 4, which contains two representations of this goddess, one on the right hand, and one on the left, each of which has seven small boars immediately below. As the inscription is dated in the 11th century A.D. we learn that the goddess *Vajra-Varâhi* must have been in favour at that time. Pandit Bhagwân Lâl describes the goddess Vasudhârâ of Nepâl as having six arms and three faces, with a car drawn by seven boars.

XVI.—INSCRIPTIONS, GENERAL REVIEW.

The history of the Mahâbodhi Temple may be roughly made out from the existing inscriptions. The short records on the pillars and coping of the railing point most distinctly to the erection of the first temple by Asoka, and thus verify the unanimous statements of the Buddhist chronicles.[1] The inscriptions on the Vajrâsan Throne at the back of the Temple and on the inner side of the coping show that the next temple was built during the rule of the Indo-Scythian princes in North-western India, to which period also the colossal figure of Buddha belongs. After this we have the records of the erection of several temples, and the dedication of statues at various periods from the time of Mahânâma, in the 5th or 6th century, down to the flourishing period of the Pâla kings in the 9th and 10th centuries. Then follows the records of the visits of Chinese pilgrims and the accounts of repairs made by Burmese missions in the 11th century, ending with the inscriptions of the Great Abbott Dharma Rakshita, in the 12th century, who erected several buildings at the cost of Asokaballa, the great king of Sapâdalaksha. The latest Buddhist records are roughly carved on the granite pavement slabs of the Temple, and belong to the 14th century.

In the very beginning of 13th century the whole country was desolated by the invasion and conquests of the Muhammadans. Mahâbodhi is not mentioned by name, nor is Nâlanda, but as the great monastery at Bihâr, or Uddandapura, was utterly sacked and all the monks killed by the invaders, it is certain that the two famous establishments of Mahâbodhi and Nâlanda could not have escaped. It must have been during the Muhammadan invasion that the gilt copper Umbrella of the Burmese Dharma Raja Guru was buried deep underground at the back of the Temple, whilst everything of value that was not secreted must have been either carried off or destroyed. To the savage iconoclasm of this irruption must be due the many headless and broken statues that are found at both places. I think it nearly certain that these famous monasteries were then sacked and desolated, and that they remained so for a long time. The first signs of returning life are the records of pilgrims who visited the old Temple in Samvat 1355 and 1359, or A.D. 1298 and 1302, and of others in Samvat 1385 and 1388, or A.D. 1328 and 1331. But these poor pilgrims were no longer able to build temples or

[1] *See* Section V. for these inscriptions on Asoka's Railing.

dedicate Stûpas in honour of Buddha, as their predecessors had done. Their records are limited to rough sketches of themselves and their offerings boldly scratched on the slabs of the granite pavement. In earlier days these scenes were represented in bas-reliefs sculptured on the pedestals of the statues, which the pilgrims dedicated. It seems probable also that their claim to the holy site was disputed by the Brahmans, as there still exists a round stone which formerly stood in front of the Temple with the feet of Vishnu sculptured on its face, and the date of Saka 1230, or A.D. 1308, carved on its side. This stone was originally the hemispherical dome of a Stûpa. The square socket hole still exists on the rounded face for the reception of the pinnacle.

From this time I believe that both the holy Pipal Tree and the Temple were appropriated by the Brahmans, although the place must still have been visited by occasional pilgrims from Nepâl and Burma. At present there is a large Brahmanical monastery, with a Mahant and upwards of 200 followers. This establishment has gradually grown from a very small beginning. Early in the last century it is said that a Bairâgi took up his residence under a tree, in the midst of the wild jungle which then surrounded the deserted old Temple. He was killed by a tiger, and was succeeded by a disciple. Others followed and acquired property until the successor of the poor Bairâgi has become the richest person in the district. In the walls of his extensive residence are no doubt concealed many architectural and sculptured treasures, which at some distant period may be brought to light. I had the luck to find a Chinese inscription, thickly coated with black dried oil and whitewash, inserted in one of the walls, and the large Burmese inscription was discovered upwards of 50 years ago in a similar position. At my first visit, in December 1861, I found a long Sanskrit inscription let into the ground with a hole bored in it, in which the lower tenon of the gate played. Several fine statues also exist both inside and outside the Mahant's residence, but these are all accessible. It is in the walls themselves that future discoveries may be made.

XVII.—INSCRIPTIONS, INDO-SCYTHIAN AND GUPTA, A.D. 150 TO 600.

The only inscriptions which appear to be coeval with the building of the Great Temple are the much injured record of a single line, carved around the upper edge of the Outer Vajrâsan, and the long record engraved on the inner face of one of the coping stones of the Railing.

All that remains of the first is shown in Plate X., fig. 11. Towards the end, on the right hand, I can read the well known words Mâta-pita—"mother and father." Of the rest I can only say that the letters certainly belong to the Indo-Scythian or early Gupta period, about the 2nd century A.D.

The letters of the second inscription, Plate XXVII., fig. 2, are much weather worn, and as they are carved on the northern or inner face of the coping of the southern railing, no sunlight shines upon them to assist the eye in copying. I published an eye copy of this inscription in Vol. III., Plate 29, of the Archæological Survey. The opening words are quite clear, and have been correctly read by Pandit Bhagwân Lal as—[1]

Kârito yatra Vajrâsana brihad-gandha-kuṭi prâsâde

"made where . . . in the Vajrâsan Great Gandhakuti Temple."

As *Gandhakuti* was the name given to the house in which Buddha had lived, so in aftertimes it would appear to have been applied to any temple in which an image of Buddha was enshrined. Farther on I read *Chandrârkatârakam*—"Moon, sun, stars," followed by Bhagavate Buddhâye; and towards the end of the first line I see the words *Vihâre* and *Buddhapratimâ*—"Statue of Buddha." As this is a long formal inscription in beautifully cut letters, I believe that it refers to the building of the "Great Temple," *Vrihad-gandha-kuti prâsâde*, and to the enshrinement of a statue of Buddha. In fact I take it to be a contemporary record describing the erection of the Great Temple itself, in the reign of the Indo-Scythian King Huvishka, in the 2nd century A.D.

On the coping there is also a short inscription in Gupta letters, but of less early date. This also was published by me in Vol. III., Plate 28, of the Archæological Survey. Pandit Bhagwân Lal ascribes it to the 4th or 5th century, of which I prefer the earlier

[1] Indian Antiquary, IX., 142.

date. It appears to be a pilgrim's record of a gift of money (*tankas*) for the supply of a lamp (*dîpa*), as stated by Dr. Rajendra Lâla.

The next two inscriptions, which I have given in Plate XXVII., are C, which is taken from the famous *Son-Bhândâr* Cave at Râjgir, and D, which is inscribed on the pedestal of the colossal Nirvâna statue of Buddha at Kasia or Kusinagara. They both belong to the Gupta period, about the 4th or 5th century A.D. As the Kusinagara statue was seen by Hwen Thsang, its date cannot be later than the 5th or 6th century A.D. It is therefore valuable for comparison with other inscriptions.

Inscription C, according to a translation made for me in 1862 by a student of the Benares College, records that a Muni named Vaira Deva, " of powerful dignity, was able " to obtain emancipation, having shut himself up for spiritual enjoyment in this " auspicious cell, a retired abode of Arhantas, fitted for an ascetic for the attainment " of liberation."[1] I note that the translator has misread the first word of the second line, which is clearly *Âchâryya*. In the following text I have given his reading in full, with the single correction of *achâryya* for *pravâryya* :--

निर्व्वाण लाभायत यस्मियोग्ये शुभेगुहे ऽर्हन्तरह प्रति ष्ठे ।
आचार्य्यरत्नं मुनिवैरदेवः विमुक्तये ऽकल्पयद् यतेजाः ॥

The Soubhândâr Cave, as I firmly believe, is the famous Sattapanni Cave in which the first Buddhist Synod was held, shortly after the death of Buddha. *See* the account of my second visit to it in 1872, in which I have gone over the whole question anew.[2]

Inscription D records the gift of the colossal Nirvâna statue of Buddha, 20 feet in length, which was enshrined in a temple at Kusinagara. The following text and translation of this record I owe to the kindness of Mr. J. F. Fleet, the well-known Sanskrit scholar :—

Deya dharmmâyam mahâ-vihâra châmino Haribalasya Pratimâ cha-ayam̄ ghaṭitâ Dine . . mâ (?) su (swa) rêna.

" This is the meritorious gift of Haribala, the master of the Great Vihâra, and this " image was fashioned by Dînê . . Sura."[3]

From the shapes of some of the letters, more especially from the turn up at the foot of the letter *r*, I judge that this inscription is not older than A.D. 400 to 500. This opinion is supported by the fact that this colossal image of Buddha is fully described by Hwen Thsang.

To this period also belong the coins of Pasupati the Rajâ of Nepâl, of which several were found in the small Stûpas during the excavations. One of these coins also was found in the temple marked K. in the map. According to my view of the Nepal chronology, Pasupati must have reigned about A.D. 400.

To the same period belongs the Buddhist creed, Plate XXVII., fig. E., which is carved beneath a Stûpa on the back of a statue of Buddha sitting under the canopy formed by the hoods of the great serpent Muchilinda. The form of the letter *y*, which occurs

---

[1] *See* Archæological Survey, Vol. I., p. 25.

[2] *See* Archæological Survey, I. 25, and III. 140, 141.

[3] *See* Archæological Survey, Vol. XVIII., 60.

twice, is decisive of its early date. There were originally four or five more lines under the creed, but I cannot make out more than a few detached letters.

Fig. F is a copy of the Buddhist creed of a later date, which is shown by the shape of the letter *y*.

Fig. G is a copy of the great stamp of Ṣaṣângka Deva, which is carved in reverse on the rock of the fort of Rohtâs. Its date must be from 600 to 620 A.D.

H is a specimen of the coins of Paṣupati of Nepal, several of which were found in the small Stûpas at Mahâbodhi.

K is a specimen of the copper plates with the Buddhist creed in mediæval letters.

I now come to two of the most important inscriptions that have yet been found at Mahâbodhi. These are not given in the Plates, as they have been published by Mr. Fleet. The longer records the building of a temple by Mahânâma, a resident of Âmradwipa, and a member of the royal family of Lankadwipa, or Ceylon. The slab was found near the temple marked H. in Plate XVIII. No. 2, which is carved on the pedestal of a broken statue, records the gift of the Sâkya mendicant of Âmradwipa, the Sthâviva Mahânâma. As the pedestal was actually found within the walls of the ruined temple marked H. in Plate XVIII., to the north of the Great Temple, there can be no doubt that this is the actual temple referred to in the longer inscription, No. 1. The interest attached to these two records lies in the fact that they may possibly be memorials of Mahânâma the author of the Mahâvanso, or History of Ceylon. This assignment, however, is not borne out by the date of the inscription in Samvat 279, which, if referred to the Gupta era, as the characters undoubtedly belong to the Gupta period, would refer the record to the later part of the 6th century. But the date of Mahânâma is already well known from his own history. He was the uncle of Raja Dhâtu Sena, the heir of Raja Mitra Sena, who was conquered and killed by the invader Pandu, in A.D. 433, when Dhâtu Sena and his uncle escaped.[1] The Raja continued to battle with the invaders until he succeeded in recovering his throne, in A.D. 459. During these 26 years nothing is said of the priest Mahânâma; but these two inscriptions found at Mahâbodhi show that he may have visited the Bodhi Tree in Magadha, where he built a temple and dedicated a statue. Of course the inscription belongs to the later Mahânâma of A.D. 318 + 279 = 597, and consequently I feel inclined to identify the first Mahânâma mentioned in the record with the historian of Ceylon.

To the earlier one I would assign the erection of the Great Monastery of Mahâbodhi. According to Fa Hian there were only three monasteries at the time of his visit, whereas Hwen Thsang describes the Mahâbodhi Sanghârâma as comprising *six* halls.[2] As he attributes the building to a former king of Ceylon, it seems to me highly probable that the actual builder may have been Dhâtu Sena, the nephew of Mahânâma.

The following translation of this important inscription is quoted from the Corpus Inscriptionum Indicarum, Vol. III., 277. published by Mr. J. F. Fleet, the able translator of so many of our old Sanskrit inscriptions. *See also* the Indian Antiquary, Vol. XV., p. 358.

---

[1] Turnour's Mahâwanso, page .

[2] *See* Giles's Fa Hian, p. 77, and Beal's Fa Hian, p. 126, also Beal's Si-yu-ki, II. 133.

Translation.

"Om! Victorious for a very long time is that doctrine, replete with fame, of the Teacher, the chief kinsman of the Sâkyas, by which, lustrous as the full moon, the inscrutable primary substance of existence, has been pervaded in all directions; by which the warriors, who are heretics, obstructive of the path of beatitude, have been broken to pieces, being assailed with the weapon of logic, [and] by which the whole treasure of religion, that had been stolen by the enemy, has been recovered for the welfare of mankind!

"May he, *Mahâ-Kâsyapa*, who is worthy of praise, protect you! He who observed the precepts of the chief saints, who practised that auspicious habit of abstract meditation, which is of the nature of a trance: who overcame the anguish of successive states of existence, whose wonderful subjugation of the passions is final emancipation, [is to be] displayed in the hand of Maitreya; [and] by whom the two pure feet of [Buddha] the saint were beheld at the time of attaining Nirvâna. His disciples endowed with a connected tradition of doctrine, purified as to [their] emotions, [and] active in compassion for existing beings, roamed at one time over the stainless country at the feet of the mountains of Lankâ; and in succession from them were born, in hundreds, disciples and disciples' disciples, possessed of the virtue of [good] character, who, without the glory of [actual] sovereignty, were the ornaments of a lofty race of kings.

"Then there was the *Sramana Bhava*, whose welfare was effected by the development " of abstract meditation; who discriminated between good and evil; who destroyed " error; [and] who possessed an unequalled wealth of true religion.

"And his disciple [was] he who had the name of *Râbulay*; after whom [there came] " the ascetic *Upasena*; then in succession [there was] *Mahânâman*; and after him another " *Upasena*, whose special characteristic of affection of the kind that is felt towards— " offspring—for any distressed man who came to him for protection, and for any afflicted " person whose fortitude had been destroyed by the continuous flight of the arrows " of adversity, extended, in conformity with the disposition of a kinsman, [even] to any " cruel man who might seek to do [him] harm; and by whose fame, arising from good " actions, the whole world was thus completely filled.

"His disciple, greater [even than himself], is he who has the excellent name of " *Mahânâman*, an inhabitant of *Âmradwîpa*, a very ocean of a mighty family; born in the " island of Lankâ; delighting in the welfare of others; by him this beautiful mansion of " the Teacher of mankind, who overcame the power of [the god] *Smara*, dazzling white " as the rays of the moon, with an open pavilion on all sides, has been caused to be made " at the exalted Bodhimanda.

"By means of this appropriate [action], let mankind, freed from attachment to " worldly things, having the condition of [mental] darkness dispelled; [and] like [the " flame of] a torch, having no adhesion [to material objects] enjoy the supreme happiness " of perfect wisdom!

"As long as the sun, the dispeller of darkness, shines in all directions with diffused " rays; as long as the ocean [is] full on all sides with its circles of waves that are curved " like the hoods of hooded snakes; and as long as [the mountain] Sumeru, the abode of " [the god] Indra, has its summits made beautiful by various jewelled slabs, in such a

" way as to be full of lustre, so long let this temple of the great saint attain the condition " of being everlasting.

"The year 279, [the month] Chaitra; the bright fortnight; the day 7."

The second inscription of Mahânâma, Plate XXVII., opens with the formula in use during the Gupta period for the record of a religious gift, I read it as follows :—

Deya dharmmâyam̃ Ṣâkya-bhikshoh Âmra-dwipa-vâsi Sthâvira Mahânâmasya yadatra punyatad bhavatu sarvvāsatmânâm uttarajnâ nivâptayestam!

"The religious gift of the Sâkya mendicant, an inhabitant of *Âmradwipa*, the " Sthâvira *Mahânâma*. Whatever religious merit there may be in this (act) let it be for " the acquisition of supreme knowledge by all sentient beings."

A translation by Mr. Fleet of this short record will be found in the Indian Antiquary, Vol. XV., p. 359, in almost the same words.

The last inscription of the Gupta period, given in Plate XXVIII., is taken from a headless statue now lying at Sherghâti. It has already been noticed by Dr. Rajendra Lâl and Pandit Bhagwân Lâl.[1] The statue was found by Major Mead in the temple marked R, when making excavations at my request around the Mahâbodhi Temple in 1863. The following revised account of it is given by Pandit Bhagwân Lâl, with whose reading I fully agree, excepting in one compound letter in the middle of the lower line, which appears to me to be *kty* and not *thy* :—

"This most ornamental, excellent, and lofty temple, constructed for the Muni " compassionating all sentient creatures, and the vanquisher of Mâra, by him named " Bodhishena, a monk, pure minded, delighting in the way of perfect wisdom, an " inhabitant of Dattgalla, for the (purpose of) unloosing the fetters of the world, of his " parents, and also of relations, and his teachers, &c., inhabitants of Ahavâgra."

Dattagalla and Ahavâgra I have failed to identify.

---

[1] Buddha Gayâ by Rajendra Lâla Mitra, pp. 192–3, and Notices of the same by Pandit Bhagwân Lâl, in Indian Antiquary, IX. p. 143.

XVIII.—INSCRIPTIONS—MEDIÆVAL.
A.D. 600 TO 1000.

There is an almost complete dearth of inscriptions during the 7th and 8th centuries, the only record that I can refer to this period being the Buddhist creed given in Plate XXVIII., fig. F, which is found on the back of a statue. There are a few letters, masons' marks, on some of the pieces of the blue basalt throne inside; but they are of common forms, and are besides too few in number to give a definite clue to their date. But they are certainly later than the latest Gupta inscriptions.

But with the rise of the Buddhist kings of the Pâla dynasty, in the beginning of the 9th century, the inscriptions are pretty numerous. Of the founder *Gopâla*, I have given one in Plate XXVIII., fig. 2. That he was a Buddhist we have the direct testimony of Târânâth,[1] who states that he built a temple at Nâlanda, not far from *Otantapura* (that is, *Uddandapura* or Bihâr, the *Adwand-Bihâr* of Muhammadan historians). His reign has been fixed on pretty sure grounds in the beginning of the 9th century, say, 800 to 825. The inscription, which was exhumed at Mahâbodhi, simply records the dedication of a statue in the reign of Sri Gopâla Deva. No. 3 of the same Plate is a short inscription of the time of his son Dharma Pâla, which was found by me to the south of the Great Temple; but was most probably exhumed during the Burmese surface clearance. It records the dedication of an image of the four-faced Mahâdeva. I made it over to Dr. Rajendra Lâl, who has published the following text and translation :—

१ । त् द्म्य (१) + श्रायनभरस्य उज्ज्वलस्य श्रिलाभिदः ॥ +
२ । श्रकास्थेन पुत्रेण महादेवश्चतुर्मुखः ॥ श्रेष्ठ +
३ । म + । म + + गङ्गायो धिमिधा सिन। ॥ स्नातक +
४ । + अच्चयानु श्रेयसे प्रतिष्ठापितः पुष्करि-
५ । ण्यत्य (च) + याचपूता विष्णुपदी समो ॥ चितरे-
६ । न सहस्रेण द्रम्माणां खानिता + ॥
७ । ष । षिंश्रति तमेवर्षे धर्म्मपाले महीभुजि
८ । भाद्रवक्रष्णपञ्चम्यां सूनोर्भास्क-
९ । रस्याहनि ॥

---

[1] Vassilief's Târânâth, p. 54, note.

Translation.

" For endless virtue, and for the good of the inhabitants of *Mahâbodhi*, an image of " the four-mouthed Mahâdeva was consecrated by Saka, the son of the noble sculptor— " Sâyanabhara (?) A tank, holy as the river, born of the feet of Vishnu, was also " excavated by him at a cost of three thousand drammas, in the 26th year of the great " king Dharmapâla, on the 5th of the wane [of Bhadra] on the day of the son of the " lord of light (Saturday)." Bengal Asiatic Society's Proceedings, 1880, p. 80. The translator, or the printer, has inadvertently omitted the name of the month, which is given in the Nâgari text as *Bhâdra-bahula-paksha*. The *dramma* was a silver coin, the descendant of the Greek *drachma*, and of the same weight. As the sum is a small one, the tank must have been a mere pond.

This mention of the week day in the inscription has enabled me to fix the date as corresponding with A.D. 850. This will place the beginning of Dharma Pâla's reign in A.D. 825. During the reign of the next king of the Pâla dynasty, named Deva Pala Deva, we have two long inscriptions, one on the pillar near Buddâl in northern Bengal, dated in the 33rd year of his reign, and the other at Ghosrâwa near Bihâr, in Magadha.[1] The latter has no date; but, as it recorded the building of a Vihâr and Stûpas at Ghosrâwa, it affords another proof of the religious zeal which animated the Buddhist community during the sway of the Pâla kings.

No. 4 is an inscription of Nârâyana Pâla Deva, who was the fourth in descent from Gopâla. He must have reigned in the early part of the 10th century, or from A.D. 925 to 950. The record is dated in Samvat 9 (of his reign), or A.D. 933, on the 5th of Vaisâkh sudi. It is of little value, except as an example of the style of letters in use at that period.

No. 5 is part of a long inscription of three lines on the base of a statue. The following is Pandit Bhagwân Lal's text and translation of this record, following the Buddhist creed.[2] There is no date.

Sindhan chchhindanvayajo vallabharâjaḥ sri ya (yu) tastasya *putro* tha Deśarâjastasyâyichchathatatsutaḥ srîmân || khyâto . . . . . . payastasyaiva susangataḥ saûghaḥ . . . . . . siddhoparaḥ Śrimân || tasya sutaḥ Sri dharmaḥ Srî samantastadâtmajastasya | Sri purṇṇbhadranâmâ putromitachandramaḥ kirttish || drâkshe *tasya purańdharî*.
yadvadana ḳamalâdvinisratâ * * || Achâryo Jayasenaḥ kumârasenâsasanadyataḥ || Srimati Uddaṇḍapure yena . . . . yainjagati krittikapunjo . . . . . . pameyatâmyâtâ || teneyam̄.
gandhakuti pratimâtritayânvitâ richitâ nyastam̄a śubhamatra . . . . mbodhilâbhakrijjagataḥ || triśaranakṛitâin nandantu samantataḥ sudhiyaḥ . . . . . ||
which may be rendered—" Born in the Chinda family, of the Sindh country, was the

---

[1] Discovered by Kittoe, and translated by Ballantyne, in Bengal Asiatic Society's Journal, XVII. 492.

[2] Indian Antiquary, IX. 143, correcting Rajendra Lal's notice in Buddha Gaya, p. 198.

"illustrious Vallabharâja; his son was Désarâja; his son Ayichcha (Aditya); his son "the beloved Sangha . . . . . . illustrious . . . . . . his son the "illustrious Dharma; his son the illustrious Sâmanta; his son was named Sri Purṇâbhadra, "whose glory is like the full moon, from whose lotus like mouth came the grapes of ". . . . . . (his) Achârya Jayasenah brightening the throne of Kumârasena, by "whom, in the prosperous Uddaṇḍapura . . . . . . whose glory was like a "mountain, made this temple (*gandhakuṭi*) with three images; may the merit of it be "for the attainment of supreme knowledge to the whole world . . . . . . This "eulogy Trisâraṇa made, may the learned approve of it."

At Buddha Gayâ I obtained an inscription of Mahi Pâla, dated in the 10th year of his reign, or about A.D. 1010. *See* Archæological Survey, Vol. III., Plate 37, fig. 5. The valuable part of this inscription is contained in the following words of the second line:—

Parama Bhaṭṭâraka, parama Saugata, Sri man Mahipâla Deva pravardhmâna, vijaya râje . . daṣame Samvatsare.

"During the prosperous and victorious reign of the supreme sovereign, the pre- "eminent Buddhist, the fortunate *Mahipâla Deva* . . in the 10th year."

Here the term *parama Saugata* distinctly declares that Mahipâla Deva himself was a follower of Buddha. It is perhaps worthy of notice that the great Temple at Nâlanda was repaired in the 11th year of the reign of Mahipâla.

No. 6 is a short undated inscription of Râma Pâla Deva, on a long slab. The exact position of Râma Pâla in the list of kings is not known. I found another inscription of him in Chandi-Mau, dated in the 12th year of his reign.[1] I have formerly placed him after Mahipâla, but I now think that he may perhaps be identified with Mahipâla's grandfather, whose name is lost, but is known to have consisted of two syllables. This identification would place him about 960 to 980 A.D. Târânâth, however, gives a Râmapâla as the grandfather of the last Pâla king, named Yaksha Pâla.

I have already quoted the title of *parama Saugata*, or "prominent Buddhist," given to Mahipâla, as a proof of his attachment to Buddhism. To this I may now add the inscription on a figure found at Sârnâth, which was first published by Wilford.[2] As it is dated in the Samvat year 1083, or A.D. 1026, we get one certain date for the reign of Mahipâla. The following version was made in 1862 by a student of the Benares College:—

"Adoration to Buddha. Having worshipped the lotus foot of Sri Dhama-râsi, "sprung from the lake of Varânasi, and having for its moss the hairs of prostrate kings, "the fortunate Mahipâla, king of Gauḍa, caused to be built in Kâsi hundreds of "monuments, such as *Isâna* and *Chaitraghanta*."

"The fortunate *Sthira-pâla*, and his younger brother, the fortunate *Vasanta-pâla*, "having renewed religion completely in all its parts, have raised a tower (*Saila*) with "an inner chamber, *garbha-kuti*, and eight large niches, in Samvat 1083, the 11th day of "Pausha."

---

[1] Archæological Survey, Vol. XI., p. 169.

[2] Archæological Survey, Vol. III., 121, and XI., 182.

The text of this inscription will be found in Vol. XI., p. 182, of the Archæological Survey. The inscription was found at the large brick mound called Chokandi, just half a mile due south of the great Stûpa of Dhamek, at Sârnâth. I suspect that *garbha-kuṭi* *must* have been an erroneous reading for *Gandha-kuṭi*.

In the end of 1861 I discovered a long inscription on a black slab at the Mahant's gateway, in which the lower tenon of the gate worked. A very good facsimile of this inscription has already been published by Dr. Rajendra Mitra, along with a text and translation. It is dated on the 5th of Srâvana in the year 15 of the reign of king *Tunga*, of the Râshtrakuta race. It is a long rambling farrago of the praises of the king and his immediate predecessors, ending in the simple statement of the erection of a *Gandha kuti*, "like unto a flight of steps to heaven." There is no date, but from the style of the letters I judge the inscription to belong to the 10th or 11th century.

XIX.—INSCRIPTIONS—CHINESE.

The intercourse between India and China seems to have begun soon after the conquests of the Great Yueti, or Tochari, in the North-west. The earliest notice that I can find is in B.C. 2, when the king of the Yueti sent an envoy named *I-tsun-keu* (Asauga ?) with a Buddhist book, in which mention was made of Bodhisatwas, Srâvanas, Bhikshus, and other Buddhists.[1] The reigning king of the Yue-ti at that time was Kujulo Kadphises, who must have been a Buddhist, as he calls himself on his coins *Sacha-dharma-thidasa*, or the "upholder of the true Dharma."

The next mention is by Hwen Thsang,[2] who states that Kanishka kept the hostages received from the neighbouring kings at *Chinapati* in the Eastern Punjâb during the winter season, which received its name on that account. These hostages also are said to have introduced the peach called *chinani*, and the pear called *Chinaraja-putra*, into India. The flat China peach, which is still common in the Jâlandhar Doâb, attests the truth of the story; Kanishka almost certainly reigned about 100 A.D.

In A.D. 159–162, the Chinese Emperor Hiwan-ti having dreamed that he saw a golden man,[3] and having learned from his ministers that a divine being named *Fo* (Buddha) was worshipped in India, sent an embassy to learn the law and doctrine of Fo, and to bring back his portrait and statue. He is also said to have sacrificed to Fo (the Buddha) as well as to Las-tsen.

During the period of the "Three Kingdoms" (A.D. 220 to 265), India is said to have belonged to the Great Yue-ti. This of course refers to North-west India only.

During the time of the Wei and Tsin dynasties (A.D. 220 to 420), the relations with India were interrupted. Once only during this time the king of Funân (222–278 A.D., or 222 to 280) sent an ambassador to India.[4] From his report we learn that Buddha was worshipped, that the king bore the title of *Meu-lun*, and the fortified capital stood on the bank of the Ganges. This was no doubt Pâtaliputra. The king has not yet been identified.

In A.D. 502, King Kiuto (perhaps Gutta or Gupta), whose family had reigned for many generations, sent an embassy to China.[5] If a Gupta king, he must have been one

---

[1] Pauthier, Journal Asiatique, 1839, and "Le *Thian-chu*, ou l'Inde.

[2] Julien's Hwen Thsang, I. 174, and II. 199.

[3] Pauthier, Journal Asiatique, Octobre, 1839.

[4] Pauthier, Journal Asiatique, Octobre, 1839, p. 285.

[5] Pauthier, Journal Asiatique, Octobre, 1839, p. 286.

of the earliest successors of Budha Gupta in Magadha, while Mâlwa and Western India were held by Toramâna.

Afterwards, during the 7th century, as we learn from the Chinese records, there was frequent intercourse between India and China, beginning with the long sojourn of Hwen Thsang, from A.D. 629 to 642. This intercourse was no doubt stimulated by the friendly reception accorded to Chinese pilgrims by the great Buddhist king Harsha Vardhana, during whose long reign, from A.D. 607 to 648, the progress of Buddhism was zealously fostered.

In A.D. 638 Yuan-chan entered India from the north-west, viâ Jâlandhara, and, after spending four years at *Mahâbodhi*, returned to China. In A.D. 665 he came back to India, and once more visited *Mahâbodhi* and the Vajrâsan throne.[1]

About A.D. 640 Hwui Lun followed Yuan-chan, and visited the Vajrâsan throne at *Mahâbodhi*.

During the 8th and 9th centuries there was little if any intercourse between India and China, which cessation was no doubt caused by the rapid progress of Brahmanism and the consequent decay of Buddhism.

The intercourse between the two countries was partially resumed during the 10th century, during the rule in Magadha of the Buddhist kings of the Pâla dynasty. In the time of Mahipâla, A.D. 1000 to 1040, numerous Chinese pilgrims visited *Mahâbodhi*, and set up memorials of their visits, some of which have lately been discovered during the course of the recent excavations around the Great Temple.

Chinese inscriptions, Nos. 2 and 3, Plate XXX., were actually found *in situ* on two slabs forming the lower part of the basement of two small Stûpas built of sandstone at the spot marked Z^1 in the plan. *See* Plate XVIII. A third inscription, No. 1, was found under the north face of the northern Samâdh Cenotaph of a Mahant. This also must have been originally close to the others, as the stone Stûpa to which it belonged is particularly stated to have been built 30 paces, or 75 feet to the north of the Bodhi Tree. A fourth inscription, No. 4, was found by myself built into one of the walls of the Mahant's residence, and thickly covered with repeated coats of whitewash. I observed a slight depression in the wall with a pointed top, and I thought that I could see traces of letters. On clearing away the whitewash this perfect Chinese inscription was discovered. A fifth inscription, in three lines, No. 5, with eight standing figures carved above, was found by Mr. Beglar.

From these Chinese records we learn that there were two great epochs of Chinese pilgrimage, the first in the 7th century, during and immediately after the reign of the powerful Buddhist king Harsha Vardhava, and again in the 11th century, during the most flourishing period of Buddhist sovereignty under King Mahipâla and his successors.

The following translations are all due to Mr. H. A. Giles, one of our consular agents in China, and a well known Chinese scholar. For the word Pagoda I have substituted *Stûpa*.

[1] Mr. Beal, in the Indian Antiquary, Vol. X., 209.

No. 1.—CHINESE.

Hymn of praise set up by the Priest Yun-shu, in A.D. 1021. *See* Plate XXX., fig. 2, for the sculptured top of this slab. The figures to the right and left of Buddha represent the goddess Vajra Varâhi. A complete copy is given in the Royal Asiatic Society Journal for 1881, Vol. XIII., p. 557.

Record of a hymn of praise in honour of the body and throne of Buddha, by the Priest Yün-shu, from the Western River (Yellow R.) of the Great Sung Empire (China), reciter of the *Sûtras* (expounder of the *Shastras*).

"I, Yün-shu, having come from my far distant fatherland [1] to gaze upon the territory " of Buddha; and then having seen with my eyes the miraculous footprint, was I not " respectfully to offer my homage in glorification of my God? I therefore collected " together what of money I could spare, and some 30 paces to the north of the Bodhidruma " I [2] raised a stone to the Ten Thousand Buddhas.

" On three occasions Chiang Hsia-pias spent here the season of fast; but he had not " the wherewithal to express his deepfelt gratitude and overflowing respect, and was forced " to content himself with eulogistic utterances upon the countenance of the birthless " intelligence. He said:—

" O great Master, merciful to the people, sympathising with all creatures,
" Although thou dost not manifest thyself, still thou art a most efficacious God.
" The herd of evil ones gaze up towards thee and recognize thy universal love
" Increasing with the changing moons of the past two thousand years."

He also said:—

" Oh, I could gaze on thy *lakshana* [3] for ever.
" The majesty of thy countenance is rare indeed;
" The crown of thy head is of fine serpentine;
" Thy eyes like lotus flowers in a pool;
" The *Swastika* [4] is written in gold upon thy breast;
" The down on thy shoulders is like threads of snow;
" Wonderful indeed is thy marvellous hand;
" The texture of thy robes is impermeable to dust and smoke."

And as Chiang Hsia-pias had hymned the shadow, I determined to pronounce a eulogium on the body, of which Buddha has three in all. And I began with the *Nirvâṇa-kâya* [5] as follows:—

" Deep is thy sympathy, genuine as the face of the moon:
" Thou hast saved mortals from out of the midst of fire:
" Thou handest down the traditions of the healing art:
" Thou stringest pearls in branching relationships.
" The Three Vehicles lead the way to wisdom.
" The five precepts brush away thy confusing dust of the world:
" Mental disturbance extinguishes the light of the intellect,
" But reaches not thy body, which is beyond the pale of matter."

---

[1] That is, having accomplished the long and dangerous journey from China to India overland.. [*See* Post.]

[2] The famous Bodhi Tree, near Gayâ, under which Shakyamuni Buddha obtained *bodhi* or enlightenment.

[3] Thirty-two characteristic marks which are found upon the body of every Buddha.

[4] The mystic symbol?

[5] That body which has the power of assuming any shape of man or animal, &c.

I then proceeded to hymn the. *Sambhôga-kaya*,[1] as follows:
" The myriad priests in the garden of *Jeta*,[2]
" Released from mortality, pass from the thraldom of desire.
" The dust of this earth is wiped away:
" They long to enter into possession of the middle kingdom.
" The body of every Buddha possesses illimitable potentialities:
" His heart is dissevered from all ties:
" Cast for ever into the sea of the *Trilŏkya*[3]
" Personal ambitions are entirely obliterated."

I finally went on to eulogise the *Dharma-kâya*[4] as follows:—
" To witness the source and wander over the sphere of the Law
" It was well to travel through dust and desert,
" Bright, bright, without beginning or end;
" Dark, dark, breaking the chain of *nidâna*[5]:
" Dwelling on earth without becoming earthy:
" Abiding in heaven without undergoing change;
" In this eulogium I utter the deepest words of my heart,
" For I have at length met with the Immaculate Body."

And when I had eulogised the Triple Body, I desired also to eulogise the throne of each body, wherefore I proceeded to eulogise the shrine of *Nirmâṇa-kâya* as follows:—
" There are wondrous footprints in the Five Heavens,
" Produced within the limits of the six cardinal points,
" In depth descending to the bottom of the golden *chakkra*[6],
" In height reaching to the surface of the earth;
" Never do any mortal cares mingle there,
" For how can fire and water blend?
" Sometimes the armies of Mâitrêya and Mâra fight,
" Until the latter are quelled by the roar of the lion."

I then eulogised the shrine of *Sambhoga-kaya*, as follows:—
" This shrine towers above the limits of the *Trilô-kaya*;
" Its shapely summit rests above the sky,
" The *Kalpa*[7] of fire exercises no influence over it;
" On earth how should we seek to model its like?
" The reputation of King Asoka extends afar:
" He rested in wonderful perception of the doctrine.
" A jewel among grains of sand,
" Immortal, he will permeate the Great Void."

---

[1] That body which represents the merit and consequent reward of every Buddha.
[2] Near Srâvasti; a favourite resort of Buddha.
[3] The regions of lust, form, and formlessness.
[4] The spiritual body of every Buddha.
[5] The everlasting chain of cause and effect.
[6] The wheel [of the law of Buddha].
[7] A great period of time.

I then eulogised the shrine of the *Dharma-kâya* as follows :—

"No beginning, no birth, no death;
"All distracting influences at an end;
"Steadily pursuing the Five *Gati*[1];
"Quietly entering into the *kalpa* of the Three Plagues[2]
"O supremest manifestation of wisdom,
"Pure essence separated from the gross,
"Even though passing through a hundred myriad *kalpas*,
"Thou wouldst still be removed far from the dust of this earth."

Thus with the most fitting of my poor language did I strive to glorify the Great Doctrine, measuring, as it were, with the eye of a mosquito, the vast expanse of sky, perceiving not the magnitude of my task, but anxious only to give expression to my heart's burden. And now I take these hymns on the Triple Body, consummate in its excellence, and cause them to be engraved, in the hope that prosperity and long life may thereby accrue to my honoured Prince, the Sovereign of the Great Sung Empire. For His Majesty is humbly desirous that the destiny of the Doctrine may resemble that of the Sacred Pool, from which nothing may be taken, and to which nothing may be added, the waves of which are liable neither to increase nor decrease; its blessedness that of the Celestial Hill, enduring in majestic loftiness. Still more does my Prince desire that in the future of this kingdom shrine may be added to shrine, and that in other lands and other ages name upon name may be enrolled among the legions of the faithful. Also that others may hymn the praise of the miraculous footprint, and cause the same to be similarly voted down and put on record.

Recorded, and set up in token thereof, this Jen-hsu year of the reign of Divine Favour of the Great Sung[3] Empire (A.D. 1021)."

In a postscript the priest Yun-shu adds the following :—

"There went with me to worship in the land of Buddha the two priests *I-ching* and "*I-lin*, from the monastery of *Established Doctrine* in the High Street of the Eastern "Capital, who each took with him a gold embroidered *Kashâya* to be hung up in the "shrine of Mahâbodhi, and each set up his own memorial tablet in perpetual "remembrance thereof."

Neither of these memorial tablets was found at the spot mentioned in the hymn, namely, at 30 paus, or 75 feet, to the north of the Bodhi Tree, but at some distance to the eastward, where they were discovered under the foundations of one of the Brahmanical Samâdhs.

No. 2.—CHINESE.

See Plate XXX., fig. 2.

"We, the Buddhist priest *I-ching* and the novice *I-lin*, from the monastery of "'Doctrine Established,' in the Eastern Capital of the Great Sung Empire, in humble "recognition of the Four Mercies and the Three States of Existence, here present one

[1] Conditions of living creatures generally enumerated as six in all.

[2] Pestilence, war, and famine.

[3] The name of the Imperial House which at that date swayed the destinies of China.

"gold-embroidered Kashâya to be spread over the throne of the Buddha of the Western "Heaven. And we have further caused to be erected a stone Stûpa."

"Recorded on a day of the 4th moon of the 6th year of Divine Favour, when the "Upâdhya *Pien-cheng* was Chief Teacher."

No. 3.—CHINESE.

See Plate XXX., fig. 3.

"I, the Buddhist priest *Yu-pin*, from the monastery of the Commencement of "Holiness, in the Eastern Capital of the Great Sung Empire, do here present one "gold-embroidered *Kashâya* to be spread over the throne of Buddha. And I have "further caused to be erected a stone *Stûpa*, in humble recognition of the 'Four "'Mercies,' and the 'Three States of Existence,' of which I have been mercifully "permitted to partake."

"Recorded on a day of the 4th moon of the 6th year of Divine Favour."

No. 4.—CHINESE.

This is the inscription which was discovered by myself concealed under numerous coats of whitewash in the wall of one of the buildings of the merchant's residence. The translation is by Mr. H. A. Giles. The date of the inscription is A.D. 1033.

A. Cunningham.

"This Stûpa (no copy in Plate) was erected by the Emperor and Empress of the "Great Sung dynasty, in memory of His Imperial Majesty T'ai Tsung."

"By command of His Imperial Majesty, our divinely enlightened, most glorious, "most virtuous, most filial, sovereign of this the Great Sung dynasty, and of Her "Imperial Majesty, our most gracious, most virtuous, and most compassionate Empress, "I the Buddhist priest, Hui-wen, have been humbly commissioned to proceed to the "country of Magadha, and to erect, on behalf of His departed Imperial Majesty T'ai "Tsung—the humane, the orthodox, the deserving, the divinely virtuous, the wise, the "supremely filial,—a pagoda beside the Bôdhimanda, the Diamond Throne. For His "Imperial Majesty, T'ai Tsung, was humbly desirous of passing aloft to the Dévalôka, "the Mansions of the Blest, there to receive the Word from Buddha himself, to witness "the ranks of the Immortal Saints, and be enrolled for ever among the ranks of the "faithful; hoping thus to secure to the House of Sung divine protection through all "generations."

"Recorded this 19th day of the 1st moon of the 2nd year of Ming Tao."

[A few remarks will be necessary to make the above intelligible to the general reader. The House of Sung came into possession of the throne of China in the year A.D. 960, and it is the second Emperor of this dynasty (A.D. 976–998) in whose honour the pagoda, or tope, or whatever the structure may have been, was set up. The term "T'ai Tsung," which may be rendered by "Venerable Ancestor," belongs to that class of titles bestowed upon Emperors after their decease; and we have therefore to look in another direction to identify the Emperor and Empress by whose commands the work was carried out. We accomplish this by referring to the date at the end of the inscription, where we read that the pagoda was erected in the second year of Ming Tao. Now Ming Tao was the second of a long string of flowery phrases by which the fourth Emperor of the Sung dynasty, quite in accordance with Chinese custom, chose to designate the years of his reign. He came to the throne A.D. 1023, and was content for the first nine years to be known under the title of *Tien Sheng*, or Divine Wisdom; but in the year 1032 he changed this to *Ming Tao*, or Manifestation of Intelligence, the word *Tao* being the term by which the Sanscrit *Bodhi* is rendered into Chinese. The designation Ming Tao only remained in use for two years; just long enough, in fact, to give us a "second year of Ming Tao," which consequently would be A.D. 1033. And that is the date of the tablet. It may be added that the devout prince who reigned under the above titles, and has since his death been known as the Emperor Jen Tsung, or Humane Ancestor, attempted to immortalise himself by the invention of a so-called alphabet for the transcription of Sanscrit words in Chinese characters, thus adding unnecessarily to an already glutted market, and making confusion worse confounded.

The "Bodhimanda" is the terrace surrounding the Bodhi Tree, or the tree of knowledge, and is said to have risen spontaneously out of the ground of a consistency as hard as diamond. Magadha, as is well-known, is the name of the ancient kingdom in which the Temple of Buddha-Gaya was situated, and is said to have been the head-quarters of Buddhism down to A.D. 400, if not later.

In conclusion, it may interest some to know that this legend, so to speak, above the inscription, is engraved in what Chinese scholars know as the "lesser seal" character—a style in vogue when the materials for writing consisted of a sharp-pointed instrument and a piece of bamboo. The invention of paper and of the hair brush brought about a revolution in the form of the written character, and the lesser seal, which held its own from B.C. 800 to B.C. 200, was subsequently used only in cases where an ornamental style might be considered desirable. The inscription itself is in the most modern style of Chinese writing which has existed since the 4th century of our era, and is a modification of a heavier style intervening between that date and the lesser seal mentioned above.] The above remarks by the translator, Mr. H. A. Giles.

No. 5.—CHINESE.

The only account that has yet been published of this inscription is a meagre notice by Mr. Beal in the Indian Antiquary, Vol. X., p. 193, with a photograph-plate. According to him it records that *Chi-I.*, a priest of the Great Han country, "having "first vowed to exhort or encourage 30,000 men to prepare themselves by their conduct "for a birth in heaven, to distribute in charity 30,000 books relating to a heavenly "birth, himself to recite as many books, then, in company with others, travelled through "India, and arrived at Magadha, where he gazed upon the diamond throne and other "sacred vestiges of his religion. After this, in company with some other priests, he "further vowed to continue his travels through India, apparently for the same purpose." Three of his companions were named Kwei-tseih, Chi-I, and Kwang-fung.

The inscription consists of three lines of Chinese characters placed beneath a row of eight standing figures, representing the seven mortal Buddhas and the Bodhisatwa Maitreya. As these sculptures are decidedly of mediæval style, the inscription cannot, I think, be older than A.D. 1000. An engraving of the stone has been published by Mr. Beal in the Indian Antiquary, and also in the Journal of the Royal Asiatic Society, from a photograph which I sent to London.

Other Chinese inscriptions once existed at Mahâbodhi, of which only a few fragments now remain. The best of these is given in Plate XXX., fig. 5, the stone being carved on both faces. On this also I see the figure of the goddess Vajra Varâhi, of whom I have given a fine specimen in the middle of the plate. This figure I dug up in 1862 in the ruins of *Kurkihâr*, or *Kukkuta-pada-Vihâra*, "Cock's foot monastery," to the east of Gayâ. It is deposited in the Benares College.

No. 6.—CHINESE.

This is only a fragment, as shown in fig. 6 of Plate XXX. The head alone is perfect, but only portions of the first two lines remain.

XX.—INSCRIPTIONS—BURMESE.

Of all the inscriptions discovered at Mahâbodhi the most interesting and by far the most important are the records of the two Burmese missions in the 11th century A.D. To them we owe the only account that we possess of the fortunes of the Great Mahâbodhi Temple, from its earliest days down to the date of the Burmese embassies. The inscription which gives all these interesting details was found in 1829 by the Burmese embassy conducted by Colonel Burney. In it there is mention of a certain *Sri Dharma Raja Guna*, who was deputed to repair the Temple. The shorter and earlier inscription of *Dharma Raja* himself is engraved on a large copper gilt umbrella, which was found by Mr. Beglar buried 8 feet under the Burmese ground level, immediately to the west of the Temple. A representation of this umbrella is given in Plate XXIX. with its two short inscriptions in Burmese and Indian characters, copied by hand and by photography. The Burmese inscription consists of one short line, and is injured by a break in the metal. The Indian inscription consists of two lines, of which the upper one is much injured on the right hand.

The Burmese inscription appears to open with a date, but I cannot read it satisfactorily. I can make out the words *Siri Dhama Radza Guru*, but the last four letters puzzle me. The date ought to correspond with that in the Indian inscription below it, but the copper is so much crushed and broken at this part that it is not possible to read the figures with any certainty.

The Indian Bengali record I read as follows :—

1. *Sam̃* 397 *Sri Dharma Râja Guru Mahâbala dânâ ganitya* . . .
2. *Sri Râṇa Saha Dena* . . .

On account of the mediæval style of the characters, the date of 397 can only be referred to the common Burmese era, which began in A.D. 638, the year 639 being the year 1 complete. The date is therefore 638 + 397 = A.D. 1035. The difference of one year between this date and the apparent Burmese date is most probably due to the injured state of the right-hand figures of the latter.

The larger Burmese inscription is carved on a black stone, which is fixed in one of the walls of the Mahant's residence. A copy of this inscription will be found in Vol. III. of the Archæological Survey, Plate XXXII. It was made from an impression which I took in 1862, when I was allowed by the Mahant to remove the stone from the wall for the purpose of clearing the letters from the accumulated grease and dirt of many years. No less than three translations of this important inscription have been published—

1st by Ratna Pâla, a Pâli scholar from Ceylon, in the Journal of the Bengal Asiatic Society, Vol. III., 214.

2nd by Colonel Burney with the aid of Burmese scholars in the Asiatic Researches, Vol. XX., p. 164.

3rd by Hla Oung, a Burmese scholar, in Dr. Rajendra's Buddha Gayâ, p. 209.

I now give the first and last of these translations side by side.

Ratna Pâla.

"This is one of the 84,000 shrines " erected by Sri Dharma Asoka, ruler of " the world (*Jambodwip*), at the end of " the 218th year of Buddha annihilation " (B.C. 326) upon the holy spot in which " Bhagwân (Buddha) tasted milk and " honey (Madhupayasa). In lapse of " time, having fallen into disrepair, it was " rebuilt by a priest named *Naik-Mahanta.* " Again, being ruined, it was restored by " Raja Sado-Mang. After a long interval " it was once more demolished, when Raja " Sempyu-sakhen-tara-Mengi appointed " his *guru*, Sri Dharma Raja Guna, to " superintend the building. He pro- " ceeded to the spot with his disciple, Sri " Kâsyapa, but they were unable to " complete it, although aided in every way " by the Raja. Afterwards Varadasi- " naik-thera petitioned the Raja to under- " take it, to which he readily assented, " commissioning Prince Pyutasing to the " work, who again deputed the younger " Pyusakheng, and his minister, Ratha, " to cross over and repair the sacred " building. It was thus constructed a " fourth time, and finished on Friday the " 10th day of Pyadola, in the Sakkaraj " year 667 (A.D. 1305). On Sunday, the " 8th of *Tachhaanmungla*, 668 (A.D. 1306), " it was consecrated with splendid cere- " monies and offerings of food, perfumes, " banners, and lamps, and pûja of the " famous ornamented tree called *calpa-* " *vriksha*, and the poor (two ?) were treated " with charity, as the Raja's own children. " Thus was completed this meritorious " act, which will produce reward and " virtuous fruits. May the founders " endure in fame, enjoy the tranquillity of " *Nirbhan*, and Arhanta on the advent of " Arya Maitri (the future Buddha)."

Hla Oung.

" Of the 84,000 shrines of the great " King Dhamma Asoka, who ruled over " Zamboodwip Island, when 218 years " had elapsed since the Lord's religion " came into existence, Payathabat, a " temple built on the spot where Buddha " took a meal, having fallen into dis- " repair by lapse of time, a *Penthagoogyee* " repaired it. When it again fell into " disrepair, the lord of the white elephant " and king of righteousness, sent, as his " representative, his teacher, Sri Dhamma " Râjguna, who was accompanied by his " disciple, Kathaba Thera. Not being " able to perform the work, although he " had made money to do it, the lord of " the 100,000 Pyoos made a priest, " Wardathi, to undertake the work, and " spared the lesser lord of the Pyoos and " prime minister, Ratha, for it. The " work was commenced on Friday the " 10th of the waxing moon of the Pyatho " month in the year 667, and on Sunday " the 8th of the waxing moon of " Tazoungmon month in the year 668, " offerings were made of pretty flags and " kookahs. Offerings of 1,000 *thinboots* " and 1,000 lights were repeatedly made. " Offerings were also made of 21 lads " regarded as children of the bosom, and " of a Padetha tree, suspended with gold " and silver flowers, cups, and cloths. " And in order that the meal offering may " be regularly observed, debtor slaves and " cows were purchased and dedicated to " the service. It is desired that this " meritorious act may be an aid to the " attainment of Nirvâna, and of a reward " of salvation at the time of Arimadeya " Buddha."

On comparison of these three translations we gather the following prominent facts in the history of the Temple.

A.—The original Mahâbodhi Temple was built by *Asoka*, on the spot where Buddha had eaten rice and milk.

B.—Asoka's Temple having become ruinous, a new temple was built by a *Penthagugyi* (*Maha-Upâsika ?*)

C.—The Temple having got out of repair, was restored by King *Thado-Mang* or King *Sado*.

D.—Having again got out of repair, the Lord of the White Elephant sent his teacher Sri Dharma Raja Guna, accompanied by his disciple the Sthâvira Kâsyapa, to repair it; but the work was not completed.

E.—Then, at the request of the high priest Varadasi, the king (lord of 100,000 pyus) deputed Prince Pyutasing-Pyu-Sakheng and the minister Ratha, who accordingly came to India for the purpose. The work was begun on Friday, the 10th of the waxing moon of Pyatho, in the Sakka-râj year 441 (Friday, 6th December, A.D. 1079), and was finished on Sunday, the 8th of the waxing moon of Tazoungmon, in the Sakkarâj year 448 (Sunday, 18th October, A.D. 1086).

These two dates have hitherto been read as 667 and 668, but, as it is certain that the second mission of Pyu-Sakheng must have followed shortly after Dharma Raja Guru's mission, there can be no doubt that the centenary numbers must be 400. I therefore read the two dates as 441 and 448, both of which agree with the week days recorded in the inscription.[1] These new readings of the dates allow a period of 6 years and 10 months for the restoration of the Temple, instead of the short period of only 10 months, according to the previous readings. We now know that the Burmese repairs extended to a complete restoration of the whole building, including the rebuilding of the pinnacle, an amount of work which must have occupied several years. A brick with a short Burmese inscription, Plate XXIX., fig. 3, was found built into the pinnacle along with several other bricks bearing the names of the masons Gopapâla and Dharma Singha, figs. 1 and 2, in early Bengâli characters. The inscriptions on these bricks are all shown in Plate XXIX.

[1] In support of my reading of 4 instead of 6 I can point to the undoubted figure 6 for Friday, the number of the week day counting from Sunday. This figure has a distinct upper limb on the right from the top of the upper stroke, which all the four figures read as 4 want. It must be remembered also that Colonel Burney and his Burmese scholars read the two centenary figures as 4.

XXI.—INSCRIPTIONS OF ASOKA-BALLA.

There are no inscriptions of the Pâla Rajas at Mahâbodhi dated in the 12th century, during which time the Buddhist religion would appear to have fallen into decay. Indeed one of the inscriptions of this century distinctly states that in consequence of the decay of the "Law [*Sâsana*] of Buddha," an appeal was made to the illustrious Asoka-balla, King of Sapâdalaksha, for assistance.[1] With his aid, and that of a local chief named Purushottama Sinha, a Gandhakuṭi or Temple of Buddha, was built in the year 1816 of the Parinirvâṇa of Bhagavat [Buddha]. As this inscription was found by me in the Temple of Sûrya, in the midst of the city of Gayâ, the Temple alluded to may, perhaps, have stood there. But as much of the building stone used in Gayâ was brought from the ruins at Mahâbodhi, it is probable that the inscription may have been taken from that place. But there is no doubt about the locality of the other three inscriptions of Asoka-balla, as they were all found at Mahâbodhi itself, one by Mr. Hathorne, one by Mr. Beglar, and the last by myself.

No. 1, Plate XXVIIIA., Inscription is dated in the year 51 of the era of Lakshmana Sena of Bengal, or in A.D. $1170 + 51 = 1157$. It consists of 13 lines of Bengali characters. The following translation is due to Pandit Bhagwân Lâl Indraji, to whom I forwarded an impression :—[2]

"Adoration to Buddha! The Great Srâmana. He it is who tells what the root is " from which virtue springs, as also what it is that chokes that virtue.[3]

"This is the virtuous gift of the great King, the illustrious Asoka-valla-Deva, an " adherent of the excellent Mahâyâna school, a great *Upâsaka*, pious at heart. May, " whatever be its merit, be for the advancement in spiritual knowledge first of my " father and mother, and after them of all beings.

---

[1] Indian Antiquary, X. 345.

[2] *See* Journal, Bombay Asiatic Society, Vol. XVI., p. 359. The correction of the name of the prince from Asokachalla to Asokaballa was made by me, and was communicated to the Pandit along with the impression.

In the transliteration of the inscription, the printer has omitted to number one of the lines, and has thus made only 12 instead of 13.

[3] This is a new rendering of the well-known Buddhist creed, "Ye dharma," &c.

"Moved thereto by the Kashmir Pandit, the honoured Chathopadhi, by the King's "Pandit Muṣala, the worthy Ṣankara Deva and the worthy Trailokya-brahma, the "illustrious King built and furnished with an image of Buddha this Prahinya Vihârî "(Bhaṭu Dâmodara, Bhatupaima, Ṣisu Raghawa, and Mahipukha ?).

"Moreover, for the offering to Buddha, the daily ration with pots, incense and lamps, "shall be given so long as the Sun and Moon shall endure, by the leaders of the Ceylon "Assembly in *Mahâbodhi*. This offering must be prepared by the cook Mâmaka, and "the good keeper and disposer Harichandra, Samvat 51 of the reign of the illustrious "Lakshmanasena having elapsed, the 8th day of the dark half of Bhâdrapada, the "29th solar day."

No. 2.—*Indian Antiquary*.—X. 341.—Inscription found by me in the Temple of Sûrya in city of Gayâ. Translation by Pandit Bhagwân Lâl. It is dated in the Nirvâna era of Buddha, 1813, on Wednesday, Kârtik badi, 1.

"1.—Obeisance to *Buddha*, the pure obeisance to *Dharma*, the bliss obeisance to the "*Sangha* (the community), the lion—for the crossing of the world ocean.

"2.—The country called Kamâ, which was full of fathomless virtues, adorned with "all kinds of comforts, and (whose population) was of beautiful dress, lay towards the "Eastern part.

"3.—In that country was a king called Jaya-tunga-Sinha, who was illustrious as the "sole lion among the crowd of elephant-like hostile kings, possessed of a mind versed "in arms and the body of the Ṣâstras, and who was distinguished by manifold marks of "courtesy.

"4.—Omitted.

"5.—His son was Kama Deva Sinha, &c.

"6.—Omitted.

"7.—His son was the illustrious Purushottama Sinha by name, whose arm makes "glad a good country, &c.

"8.—Omitted.

"9.—Now he, with devotion, has constructed this *Gandhakuṭi* of Buddha, graceful "and like a hall of emancipation and bliss, for the spiritual benefit of the pious Mânikya "Sinha—the son of his daughter Ratna Sri, departed, as it were, to see the sublime "Jinapura (heaven).

"10.—The ascetic Dharma-rakshita, residing here as overseer (*adhishthâya*), who is "splendid, versed in myriads of sciences, very attentive, possessed of complete "knowledge (*nishṭhâ*), celebrated as the spiritual teacher of the king of the country of "Kamâ (Kumâün?), an ornament to the circle of the world (he during the erection) "carried on the work (*Karmantâram nirmane*) of this (*Gandhakuṭi*) the appearance of "which by its constant lustre removes the darkness of hell.

"11.—He (Purushottama Sinha) also having himself bowed to, and by his noble "qualities besought the illustrious *Asoka-balla*, the crest jewel of the kings of the "*Sapâdalaksha* Mountains, (and) here the Indra-like *Chhinda* King—the religion of the "Muni having decayed, effected a restoration of (or by) order—highly wonderful in this "age of strife (*Kali*) difficult to be overcome.

"12, 13, 14, omitted.

"15.—The chief of scribes, the handsome *Indranandin*, wrote it, and by the lovely "engraver Râma, it was cut in letters. Bhagavat having died in the year 1813, in the "dark half of the month of Kârtika, the 1st day, Wednesday."

The mention of Asoka-balla's name in this inscription enables us to fix very nearly the date of Buddha's Nirrâna, as accepted in N. India in the 12th century A.D. The previous inscription, No. 1, is dated in the year 51 of the Lakshmanb Sena era, and the following inscription, No. 3, is dated in the year 74 of the same era. These dates referred to A.D. 1106, give A.D. 1157 and 1180; and as Bihar was conquered by Bakhtiâr Khilji in A.D. 1198, Pandit Bhagwân Lâl has suggested that the Pegu era of B.C. 638 was probably the accepted date of the Nirvân. Deducting 638 from 1813 we get A.D. 1175 as the date of the inscription, which falls in the middle of the reign of Asoka-balla.

The country of *Sapâdalaksha*, or "One lakh and a quarter" of hills, was known to the early Muhammadans as *Sawâlak*, of which Hânsi was the capital. It included Mandor, the old capital of Jodhpur, and also Sakambhari or Sâmbhar. Asoka-balla himself was a contemporary of Prithwi Raja, the Châhumân Prince of Ajmer, who had succeeded his father-in-law Anangpâl on the throne of Delhi. I conclude that Asoka-balla was the Raja of Hânsi.

No. 3.—*Indian Antiquary*.—X. 346.—Inscription found near the Great Temple by Mr. Hathorne. Translation by Pandit Bhagwân Lâl.

"Hail to Buddha!—This is the meritorious gift of *Sri Sahaṇasâna*, son of Mahataka "Sri Mrisibrahma, a follower of the excellent Mahâyâna school, a great worshipper, a "lamp of the assemblies of Kshattris, in conduct firm like the Bodhisatwas, an observer "of truth and of vows, who was a treasurer and dependent of the Prince Daṣaratha, the "younger brother of the King *Asoka-balla*, king of kings, lord of the Khasa kings of

" the *Sapâdalaksha* Mountains, who toils like a bee on the pollen of the lotus-foot of
" Jinendra, a destroyer of the power of kings, a mounted Nârâyana of kings, a lion to
" the intoxicated elephant-like hostile kings, a father of all kings, adorned with these
" and all other such eulogistic titles of his. Let whatever merit may be in this, before
" the attainment of the fruit of supreme knowledge by the whole multitude of all sentient
" beings, giving precedences to the *Achârya, Upâdhyâya,* mother and father. In the
" expired reign of the illustrious Lakshmana Sena Deva, Samvat 74, on the 12th day of
" the dark half of Vaisâkha, Thursday."

XXII.—INSCRIPTIONS ON PAVEMENT SLABS.

There are many inscriptions roughly cut on the granite pavement slabs, both inside and outside the Temple. They are the simple records of pilgrims of a late date; but they are of interest, as they continue the history of the Temple in its fallen state long after the Muhammadan conquest. Most of them belong to the 14th century of the Saṃvat era, ranging from S. 1359 to 1388, or from A.D. 1302 to 1331. But there are a few of an earlier date, of which the best specimen is given in No. C of Plate XXVIII., it contains 21 lines, with the name Sri *Asoga-balla-Deva* in the eighth line.

In Vol. I. of the Archæological Survey, Plate VI., I published two of these pavement slab records with the dates of S. 1385 and S. 1388. On the first, which I will call A, there are five figures, all kneeling in the Burmese fashion and holding out offerings of flowers to a Stûpa. Three of the figures are male and two female. The most prominent man is called *Thâkur* (name illegible), and his wife, who is kneeling behind him, is named *Thâkurîn Jajora Devi*. The other inscriptions are too much injured to be read. The second slab has four figures, three male and one female, all kneeling and offering flowers.

On a third slab, C, there are two figures, man and wife, the former labelled *Râchrâ*, and the latter *Singâra Dabu*.

On a fourth slab, D, there are three figures, a man, a woman, and an animal, very like a dog. The man is labelled *Sundara Varma*, the woman *Nâgala Devi*, and the animal *Bhutamâna*.

On a fifth slab, E, without any figures, there is a rather neatly incised record of 10 short lines, as follows :—

Namo Budhaya
Parvatâgata Pandi-
-ta Jina Dasake-
-na Sri man Mahâbodhi
Bhandâraka darsana
Kritam yadatra punyam ta-
-d bhavati Mâta-pit
-tri purvaga sam
etat punyam likhâ-
-pitam || samvat.

"Glory to Buddha! By Pandit Sri *Jina-Dâsaka*, from the hills, adoration was made at the Temple of *Sri-man Mahâbodhi*, for the benefit of his father and mother, &c. The date was never engraved.

On a sixth slab, F, containing seven lines, and dated in S. 1359 Ashâdha Sudi 15, the pilgrim offers his adoration to *Mahâbodhi*, for the benefit of his father and mother.

On a seventh slab, G, of six lines of the same date, another pilgrim records his adoration to *Mahâbodhi* in almost the same words as the last.

On an eighth slab, H, of 12 lines, dated in S. 1365, another pilgrim records his devotions at *Mahâbodhi.*

The persistence with which all these pilgrims proclaim their devotion to *Mahâbodhi* amply justifies the title which I have given to this book. In page 3 I have quoted the statement of the Chinese pilgrim Hwen Thsang that the Temple was called the *Mahâbodhi Vihâra*, and the Monastery the *Mahâbodhi Sanghârâma.* The same name is used by all the Chinese pilgrims who visited the place in the 7th and 8th centuries. It is found in the inscriptions of Raja Asoka Balla in the 12th century, and in all the pilgrims' records on the pavement stones during the 14th century. Lastly it is used by the Ceylonese pilgrim Edmund Goonaratna, who in *Buddha-wasse* (or Buddha varshe) 2427, or A.D. 1884, recorded his visit, *Mahâbodhi pûjâya*, on a slab of white marble.

APPENDIX A.

ARCHES AND VAULTS.

Formerly it was the settled belief of all European enquirers that the ancient Hindus were ignorant of the Arch. This belief no doubt arose from the total absence of arches in any of the Hindu Temples. Thirty years ago I shared this belief with Mr. Fergusson, when I argued that the presence of arches in the great Buddhist Temple at Buddha Gayâ proved that the building could not have been erected before the Muhammadan conquest. But during my late employment in the Archeological Survey of India several buildings of undoubted antiquity were discovered in which both vaults and arches formed part of the original construction.

Perhaps the most interesting example is the vaulted chamber enshrining the colossal statue of the Nirvâna Buddha at Kusinagara. As this statue was seen by Hwen Thsang in A.D. 637, the use of the arch was certainly both known to and practised by the Hindus at that time.

A still earlier example was discovered in a mound at Nongarh on the Kiyul River, a few miles from the Lakhi Serai Station of the East Indian Railway. I found the upper half of the mound to be the ruins of a large Stûpa, which yielded only some unburnt clay models of Stûpas. At the foot of the mound I found the lower half of a life-size statue, with the remains of an inscription in old characters of the Gupta period. The excavation was afterwards continued by Mr. J. D. Beglar, who found that the horizontal layers of bricks forming the Stûpa ceased at 8 feet below my lowest work, or at 25 feet from the top, and 20 feet above the ground. Below the horizontal courses was found a small square chamber, covered by a vaulted roof formed of bricks laid edge to edge instead of face to face, exactly in the same fashion as in the vaults and arches of the Mahâbodhi Temple. As the bricks of this chamber were of much larger size (14¾ in.) than those of the Stûpa which were only 12 inches, there could be no doubt that the lower building must have been a Temple of an earlier date than the Stûpa above it. As the Stûpa itself was in ruins, and as no Stûpas were built after the Muhammadan conquest, the Temple must be older by several centuries, more especially as it must have been in ruins before the Stûpa was built over it. As the broken statue most probably belonged to it, the vaulted chamber must be also assigned to the Gupta period.

The great brick Temple at Bhitargaon, near Cawnpore, which also belongs to the Gupta period, has a vaulted entrance passage and a vaulted roof covering the sanctum. The fine old brick Temple at Barnârak in Shahabad, near the Son River, which is undoubtedly of the later Gupta period, also possesses a vaulted roof.

But though it must be admitted that the voussoir arch was known to the Hindus in early times, yet like the Greeks they seem to have made no use of it in their stone temples and to have been very sparing in their use of it in their earliest brick temples. In the case of the Mahâbodhi Temple I am satisfied that the arches and vaults which we now see did not form part of the original construction. This conclusion is based on the following facts:

I. The upper part of the great opening in the front of the Temple shows two straight sloping sides formed by courses of overlapping bricks, which lines when produced downwards to the floor of the second storey form an isosceles triangle of which the base is the breadth of that room. Now in the middle of this opening there is a cross wall, pierced with one arched doorway and two other arches a little above it. The doorway of course was the entrance to the room; but what was the object of the two arches above it, and why was not the great triangular opening spanned by an arch? I believe that this cross wall with the two arches above the door, must have been an afterwork for the purpose of giving support to the sloping walls of the great triangular opening.

II. The sanctum of the basement storey, where the statue of Buddha is enshrined, has a vaulted roof resting on two side walls which have reduced the breadth of the room from 20 feet 4 inches to 13 feet 4 inches. As the sanctum of all Hindu Temples is usually square I guessed long ago that these side walls were an afterwork for the support of the vault. This guess was verified on examining the granite pavement of the floor, as the two walls were found to rest on the flooring slabs, which had been tilted up by the great weight thrust upon them. The walls of the vault had in fact no foundation whatever, and were simple additions built upon the previously existing pavement.

III. These side walls supporting the vaulted roof are also built of smaller bricks (12 × 2·66 inches) than those of the main walls of the Temple (15 × 3 inches), and this difference of thickness of course precluded the walls of the vault from being bonded with the walls of the Temple. This want of bond coupled with the want of foundation is quite sufficient to prove that the vault could not have formed part of the original construction. I conclude therefore that this vault as well as that in the upper chamber were added to give stability to the lower part of the building, which most probably at a very early date had already shown signs of weakness in both sides of the great front opening. In fact the construction of the Temple with overlapping courses of bricks was essentially faulty, as the pressure of the lofty leaning walls had a natural tendency to thrust them inwards. This tendency may have shown itself early, and I conclude that the two vaulted chambers and the cross wall of the second storey were built with the special purpose of counteracting this inward pressure.

The great Nâlanda Temple, which was 200 feet high, certainly failed from the falling inwards of the upper half of the building. The lower part, still upwards of 60 feet in height, is now standing, but the whole of the interior was filled with the ruins. As the greater mass of the mound of ruins was to the front of the entrance, I conclude that the side walls of the great triangular opening must have given way under the enormous pressure of the lofty walls above them.

In the Mahâbodhi Temple there are three different kinds of arches used, two of which are pointed and one semicircular. The last is found only in the small spans of the narrow staircases. Its voussoirs are arranged face to face as in European arches. But the pointed arches are quite different, as their voussoirs are placed edge to edge, and not face to face. It is this difference in the arrangement of the voussoirs that distinguishes the Indian style of arch from all others. In the Mahâbodhi Temple there are two different arrangements which may be called respectively the Indian "Bondless Arch" and the Indian "Bonded Arch."

The *Bondless Arch* is used only for small spans, as seen in the three small openings of the second storey of the Temple. The *Bonded Arch* is used in the greater span of 20 feet, which is seen on both sides of the three small openings. In the first kind the vault consists of a succession of thin pointed arches, only one brick thick, which simply touch each other face to face without any connecting bond. This form is still in use both in Bengal and in the Punjab for culverts and small drains. It is essentially a weak construction, as the different layers of single brick arches are liable to peel off and fall away. This fault must have become known to the Hindus very early when they adopted the *Bonded Arch*, in which two courses of bricks are laid face to face alternately with each course of the end-to-end voussoirs.

Specimens of both these kinds of arch are seen in the accompanying Plate XXXI. of the front of the Temple. Above them all is seen the upper part of the original triangular opening made by overlapping the courses of bricks on both sides until they met. A portion on each side of the opening still remains unbroken showing the overlaps.

In the front opening there was an overlap of each course of bricks. But in the walls of the Temple itself, where the slope was not required to be so rapid, the laps began after every five courses in the second storey, and after every four courses in the third storey. In this way the breadth of the floor of the third storey was reduced to 17 feet 2 inches. This storey was roofed with thick slabs or beams of wood, which formed a perfect bond connecting all four walls of the temple.

APPENDIX B.

GROUND PLAN OF TEMPLE.

On a consideration of the dimensions of all the different parts of the Mahâbodhi Temple I believe that the ground plan was laid out, after the usual Hindu fashion, on a diagram of squares. As well as I could ascertain, the side of the square, or modulus, was about 6 feet 9 inches. This was one of the ancient measures of India known as the *dhanu* or *daṇḍa*. The former was the "bow," and the latter the "staff" or bambu *lâthi*. Both were in common use among the people, and formed part of the well known scale of Indian measures. All measures were originally natural objects, and the principal Hindu measures of length are the same now as they were two thousand years ago. According to various authorities of different dates the scale was as follows:—

Angulas or Fingers.	Muths or Palms.	Hastas or Cubits.	Dhanus or Bows.	Krosa or Kos.	——	Feet.	Inches.
1	–	–	–	–	Angula = Finger	′ 0	″ 0·8437
4	1	–	–	–	Mushti = Fist	0	3·375
24	6	1	–	–	Hasta = Forearm	1	8·250
144	24	4	1	–	Dhanu = Bow	6	9·000
		4,000	1,000	1	Krosa = Kos -	6,750	—

The ruling measure, or modulus, of the Mahâbodhi Temple, as derived from the different parts of the building is about 6 feet 9 inches, which would give a cubit of 20·25 inches, and a *kos* of 6,750 feet, or a little more than one mile and a quarter [6,600 feet]. That this was an approximation to the measure of the ancient *kos* we know from a statement of Megasthenes, that "the Indians on their roads set up pillars at every 10 *stadia* to show the by-roads and distances." On this passage Schwanbeck remarks, "it seems certain that the 10 *stadia* are equal to some Indian measure which cannot be a smaller one than the *krosa* or *kos*." This measure I identified long ago with the short kos of N.W. India, which is just double of that noted by Hwen Thsang in A.D. 640, as consisting of 500 *dhanus* or "bows," the *dandas* of other authorities. It is also just one half of the great *kos* of 2,000 *dhanus*, the common *kos* of the Gangetic provinces. Taking the *stadium* at 625 Roman feet, or 606·75 English feet, the 10 *stadia* would be equal to 6067·5 feet. Of course the 10 *stadia* were not an exact measure of the Indian *kos*, but only a useful approximation, just as we reckon 2 English miles to the large or double *kos*.

As a matter of fact, the measures of India have remained almost unchanged for upwards of 2,000 years. Such as they were in the time of Asoka, such they were in the times of Hwen Thsang and of Akbar, and such they are at the present day. Many of the *Kos-Minârs* of the Mogul Emperors are still standing on the old high road leading "from Agra to Lahore of Great Mogul." Sir Henry Elliot obtained from the revenue surveyors several measures of the distances between these Minârs. Five separate measurements between Agra and Delhi gave an average of 4,487 yards for the direct distance. As these Minârs are one great *kos* of 2,000 *dhanus* apart, the smaller *kos* of 1,000 *dhanus* would be just one half, or 2,243·5 yards, or 6,730·5 feet. I have myself measured several distances between the Minârs on the road from Delhi to Lodiana. My note books are now lost, but I remember that they all gave about 6,700 feet as the half kos. This kos is still known as the *Bâdshâhi* or *Royal kos*. The kos of 500 *dhanus*, noted by Hwen Thsang must be what is now called the *Gao-kos*, or the distance to which a cow's lowing can be heard.

The measure which I have assumed as the modulus of the plan on which the Mahâbodhi Temple was built is perhaps best represented by the monolith pillars of the stone colonnade, or Buddhist railing which surrounded the Temple. Four well preserved examples gave an average of 6 feet 9½ inches. A few measured nearly 7 feet, but as some part near the foot of each was rough, a few inches of each must have been sunk in the brick plinth on which they stood.

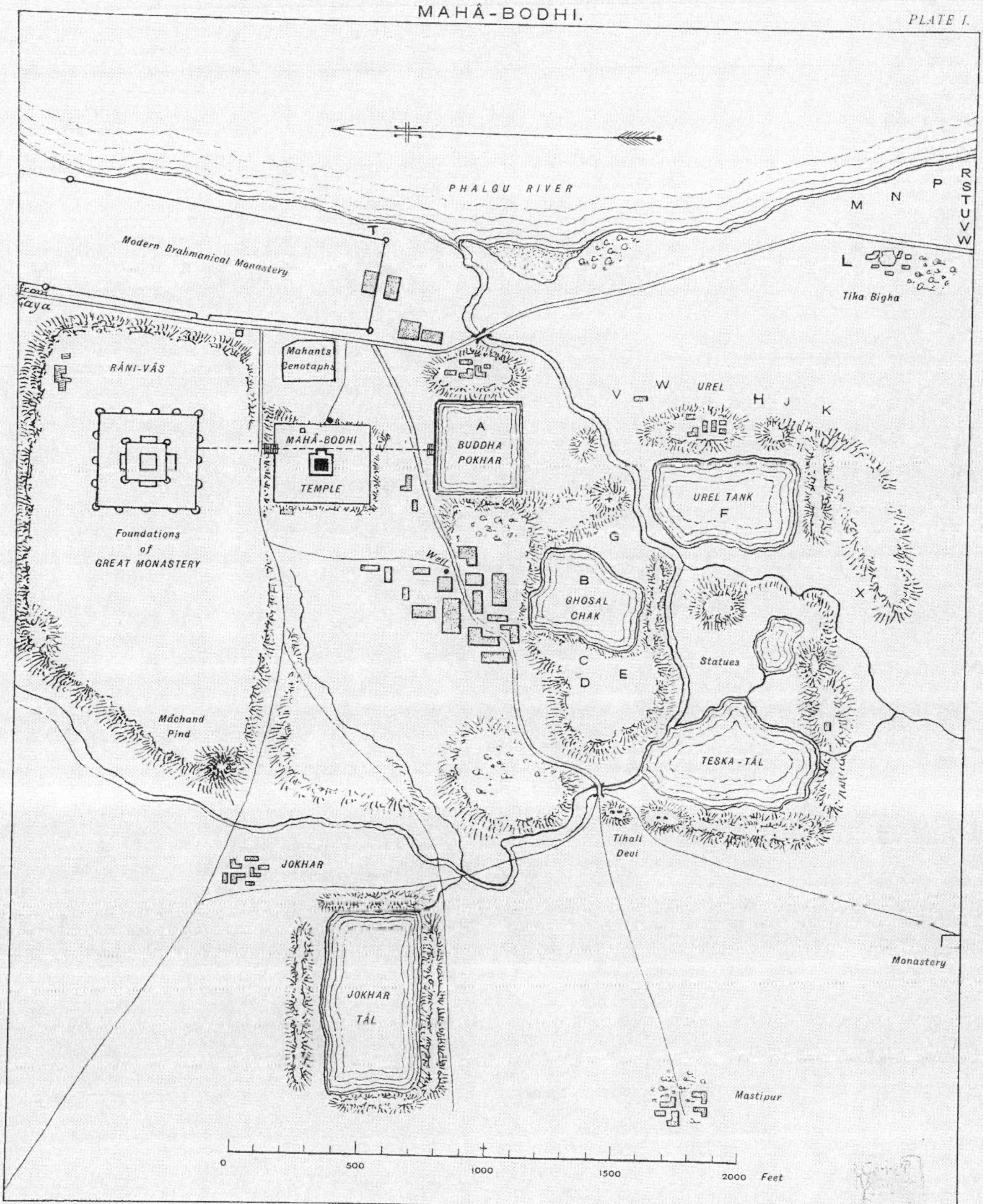

A. Cunningham, del.

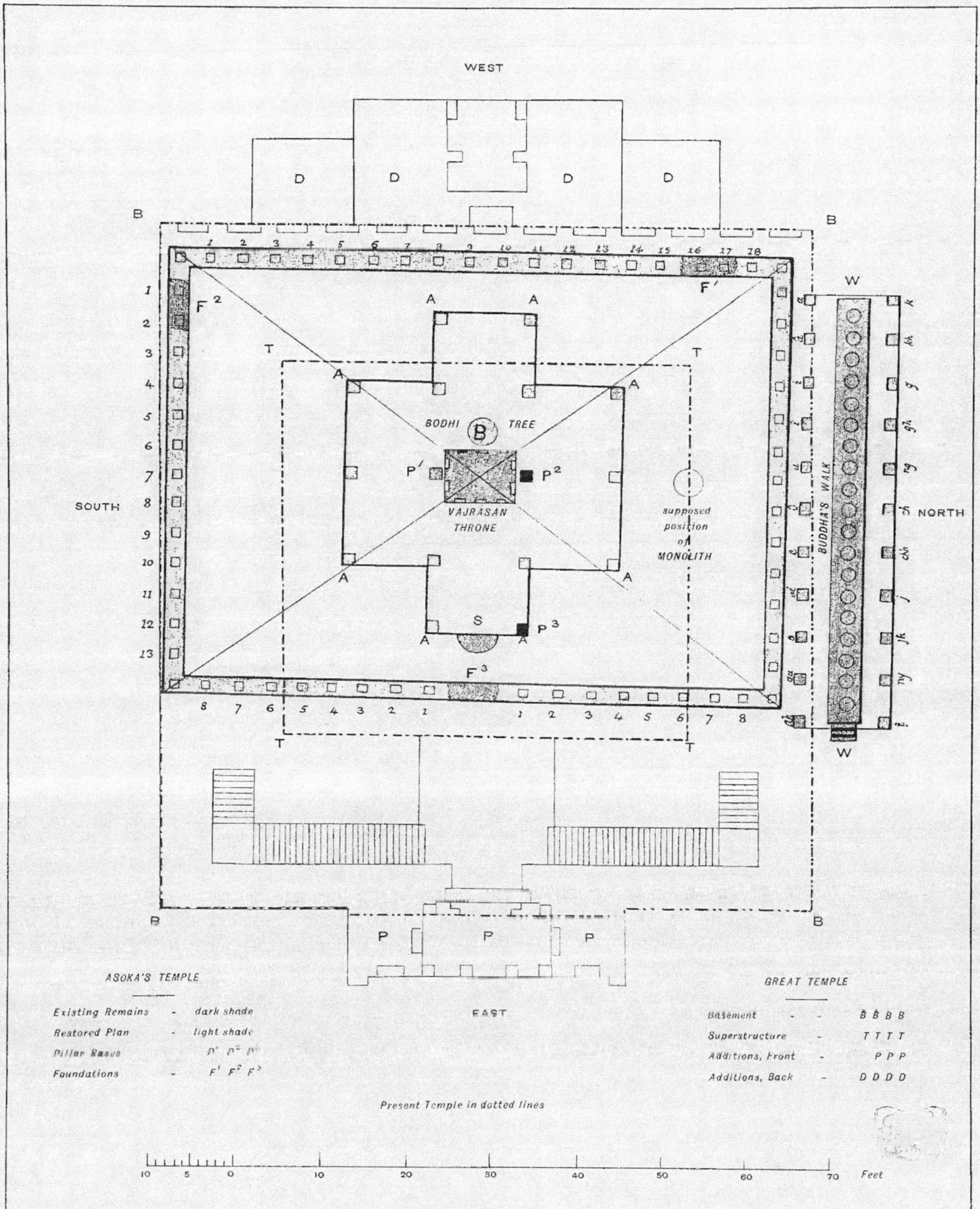

A. Cunningham, del.

MAHÁ-BODHI.

BHARHUT BASRELIEF

Inscribed
BHAGAVATO
SAKA-MUNINO BODHI.

BHARHUT BASRELIEF

A

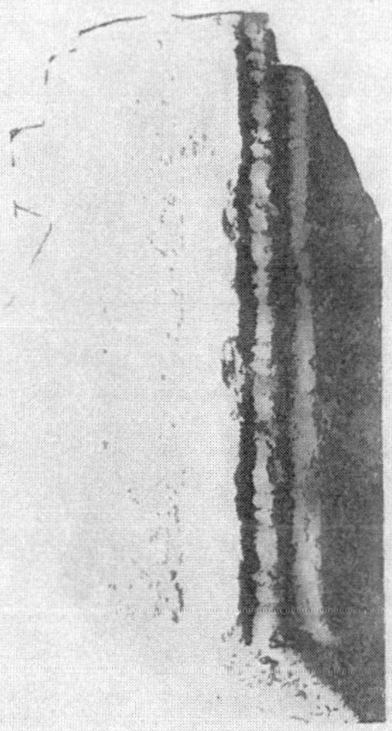

ARCHITRAVE

B

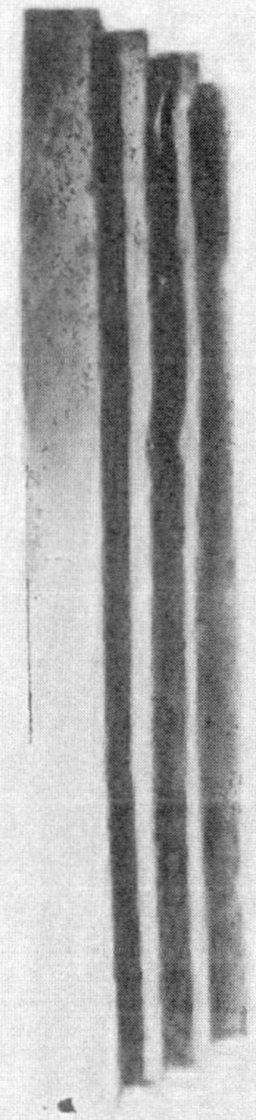

ON GATEWAY PILLAR

ON GATEWAY PILLAR

MAHÂ-BODHI.

BASRELIEF *from* BHARHUT STÛPA

REMAINS *of* BUDDHA'S WALK, MAHÂ-BODHI

PLAN *of* BUDDHA'S WALK, MAHÂ-BODHI

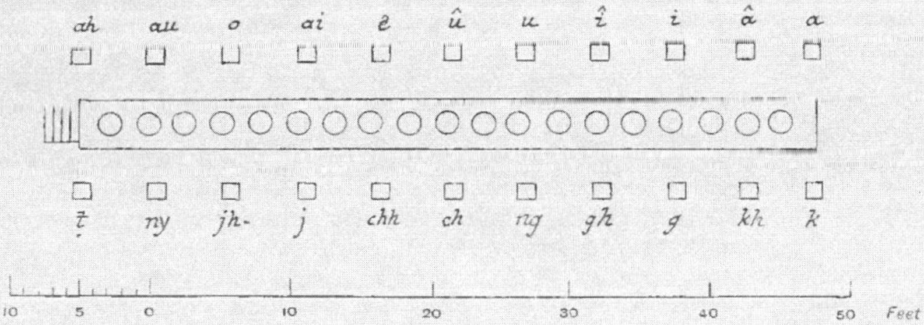

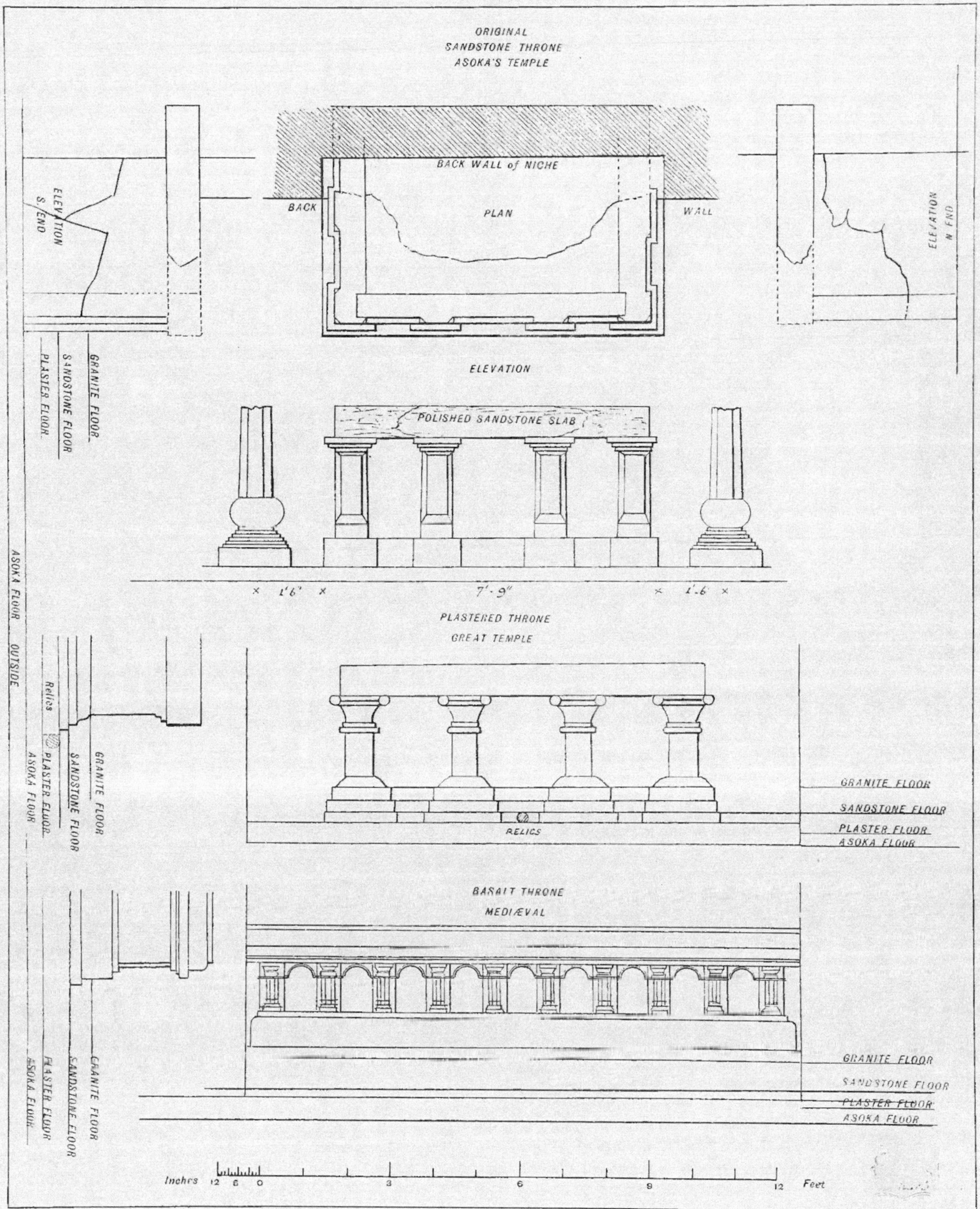

A. Cunningham, del.

RAILING OF COURT YARD.

MAHÂ-BODHI.

SOUTH RAILING
OUTER SIDE

SOUTH RAILING
INNER SIDE

END FIGURE
ENLARGED

1

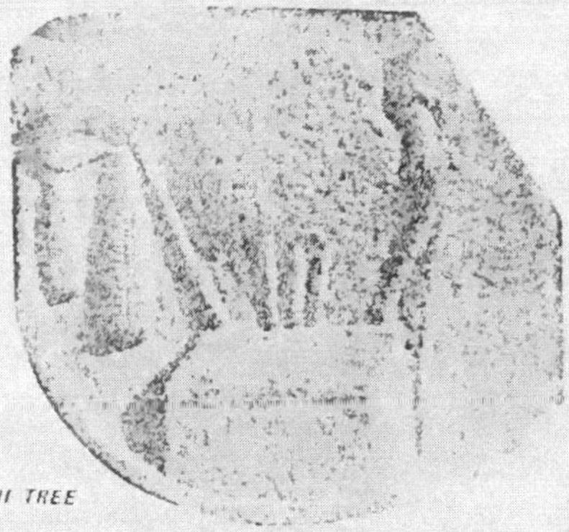

BODHI TREE

2

TRI-RATNA SYMBOL

3

DHARMA — CHAKRA

4

KALPA-DRUM

5

6

INDRA-SÂLA CAVE

7

LAKSHMI

8

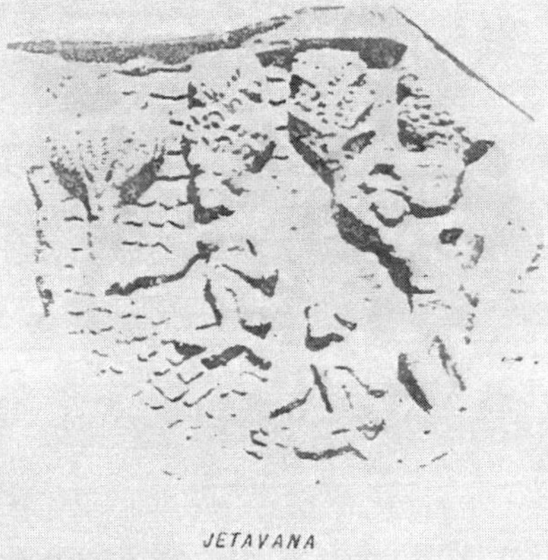

JETAVANA

9

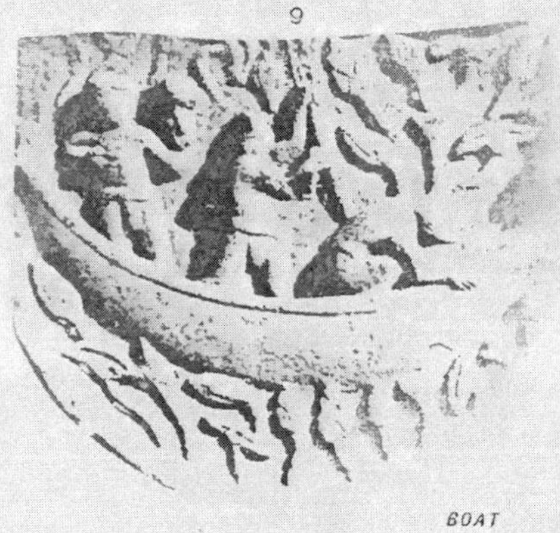

BOAT

10

11

PLOUGHING SCENE

13

1
2
3
4
5
6
7
8
9
10
11
12
13
14
15
16
17
18
19
20
21
22
23

LETTERS ON PILLAR BASES

1

ON RAIL BAR

2

ON RAIL BAR

3

ON PILLARS OF RAILING

4

5

6

7

ON COPING OF RAILING

8

THE SAME FROM AN IMPRESSION

9

DUPLICATE COPING STONE IN INDIAN MUSEUM

10

OUTER VAJRÂSAN

11

MAHÂ-BODHI. PLATE XI.

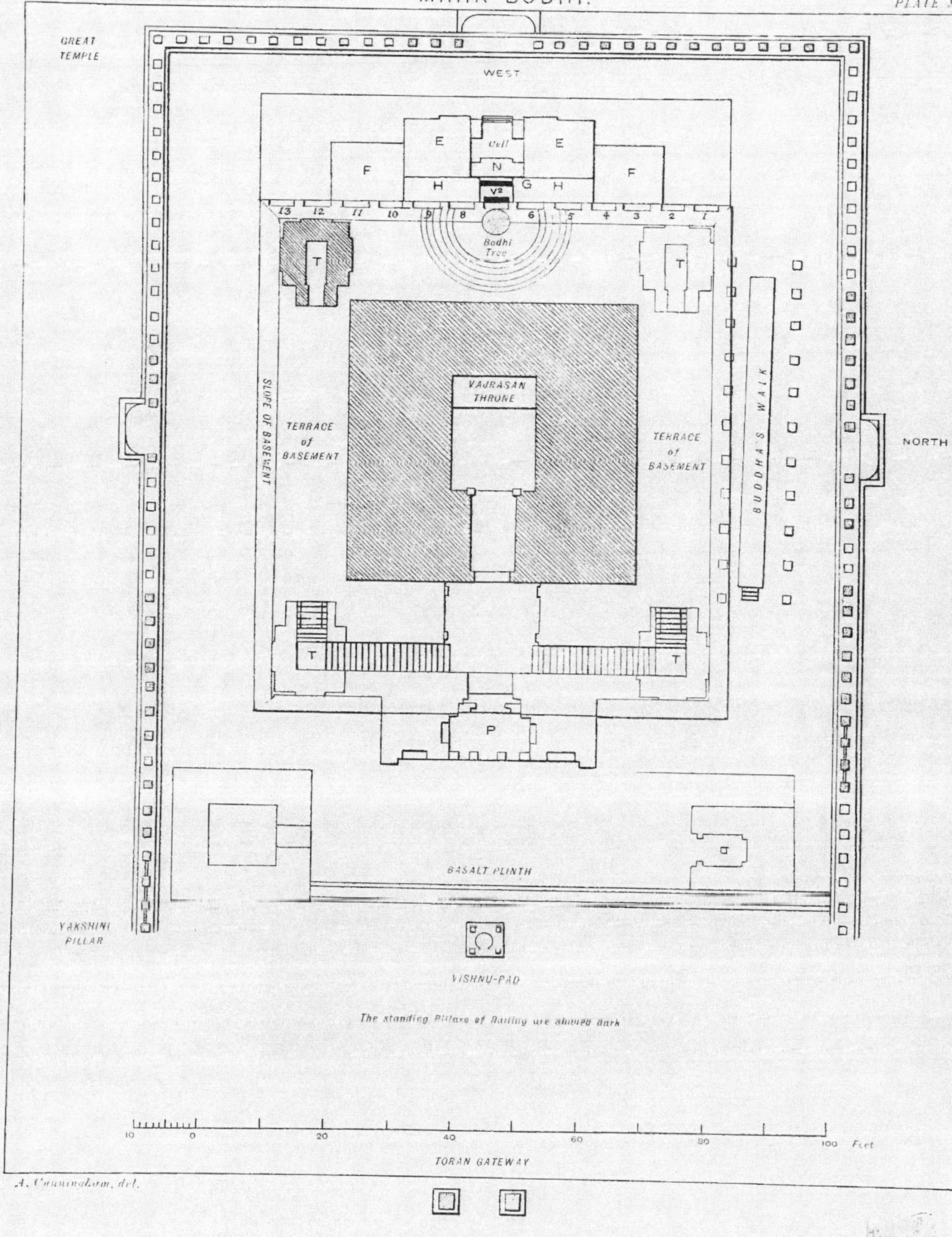

The standing Pillars of Railing are shown dark

A. Cunningham, del.

A ADDITIONS PARTLY REMOVED

B ADDITIONS WHOLLY REMOVED
SHOWING ORIGINAL 13 NICHES

A

B

MIDDLE NICHE
original figure

NEW STATUE, MIDDLE NICHE

OUTER VAJRÁSAN THRONE
AND GRANITE FACING

MODEL of TEMPLE found in EXCAVATION

WEST

BACK

NORTH

← Tree →

SOUTH

EAST

FRONT

PLAN OF MODEL

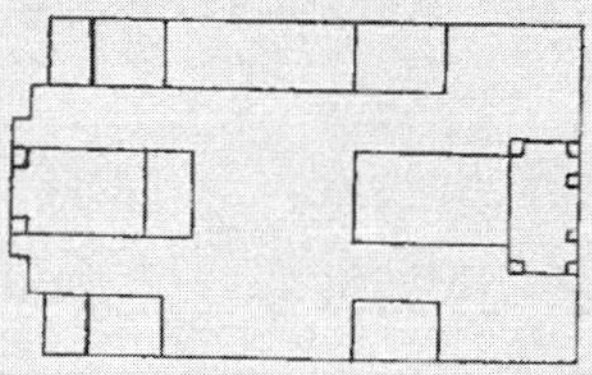

PLAN OF TEMPLE

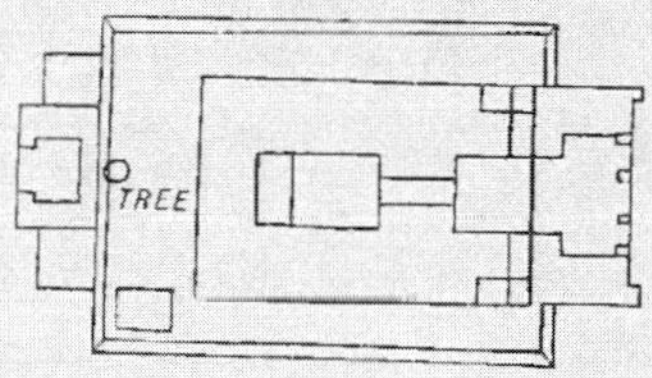

VIEW of RESTORED TEMPLE from N E.

MAHÂ-BODHI.

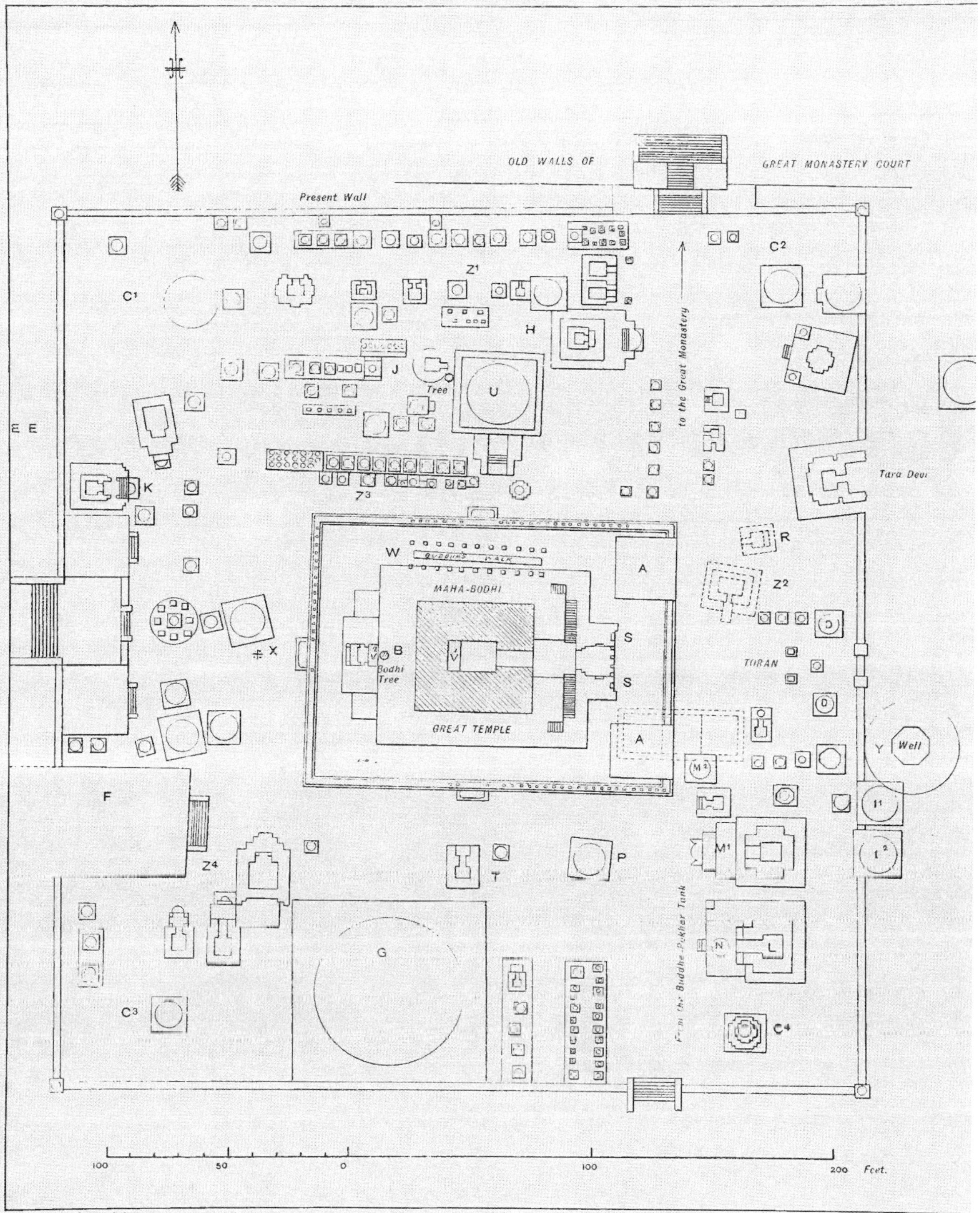

A. Cunningham, del.

COURT-YARD OF TEMPLE, N.W. CORNER MAHÂ-BODHI. *PLATE XIX.*

PLAN OF MONASTERY. MAHÂ-BODHI. *PLATE XX.*

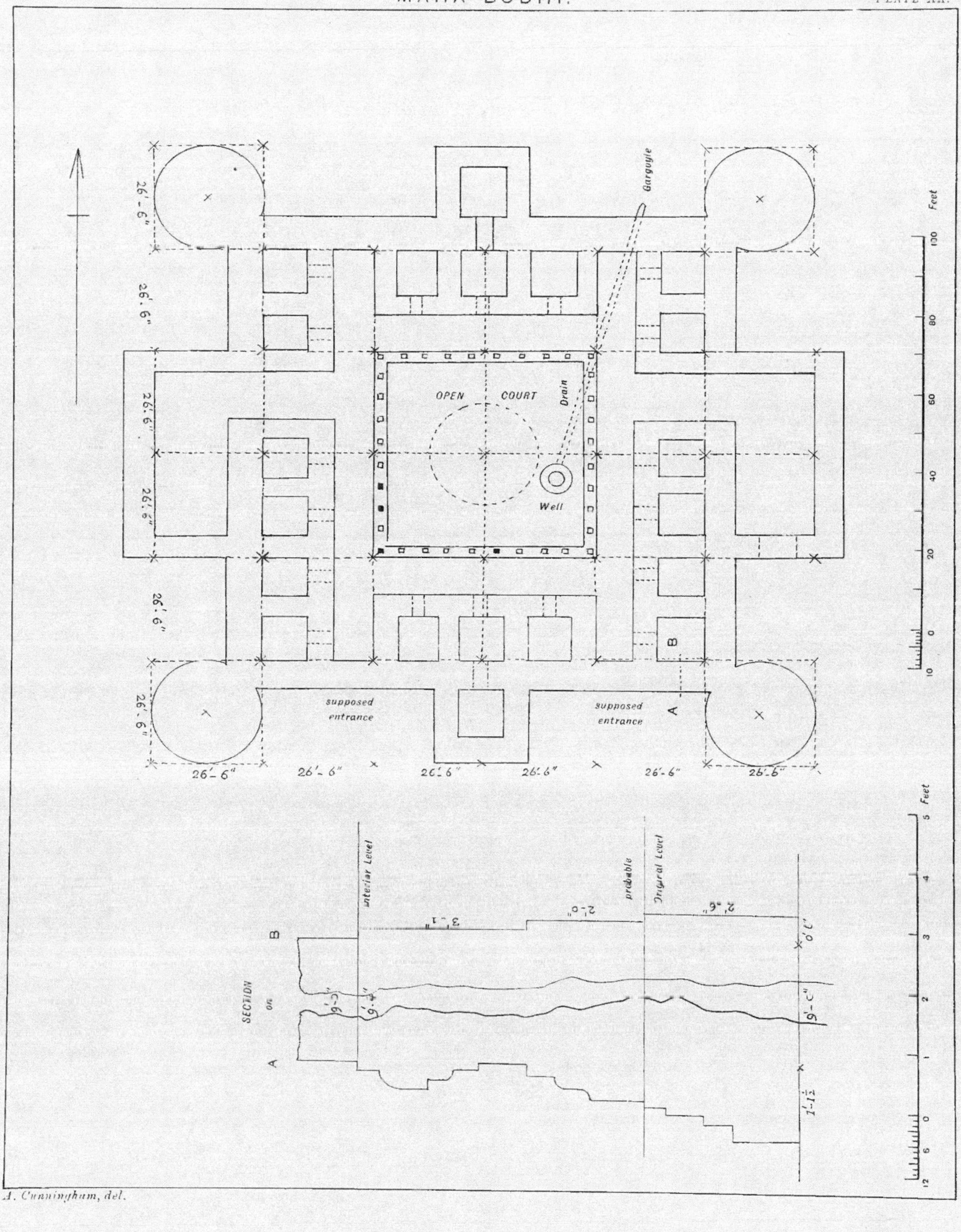

A. Cunningham, del.

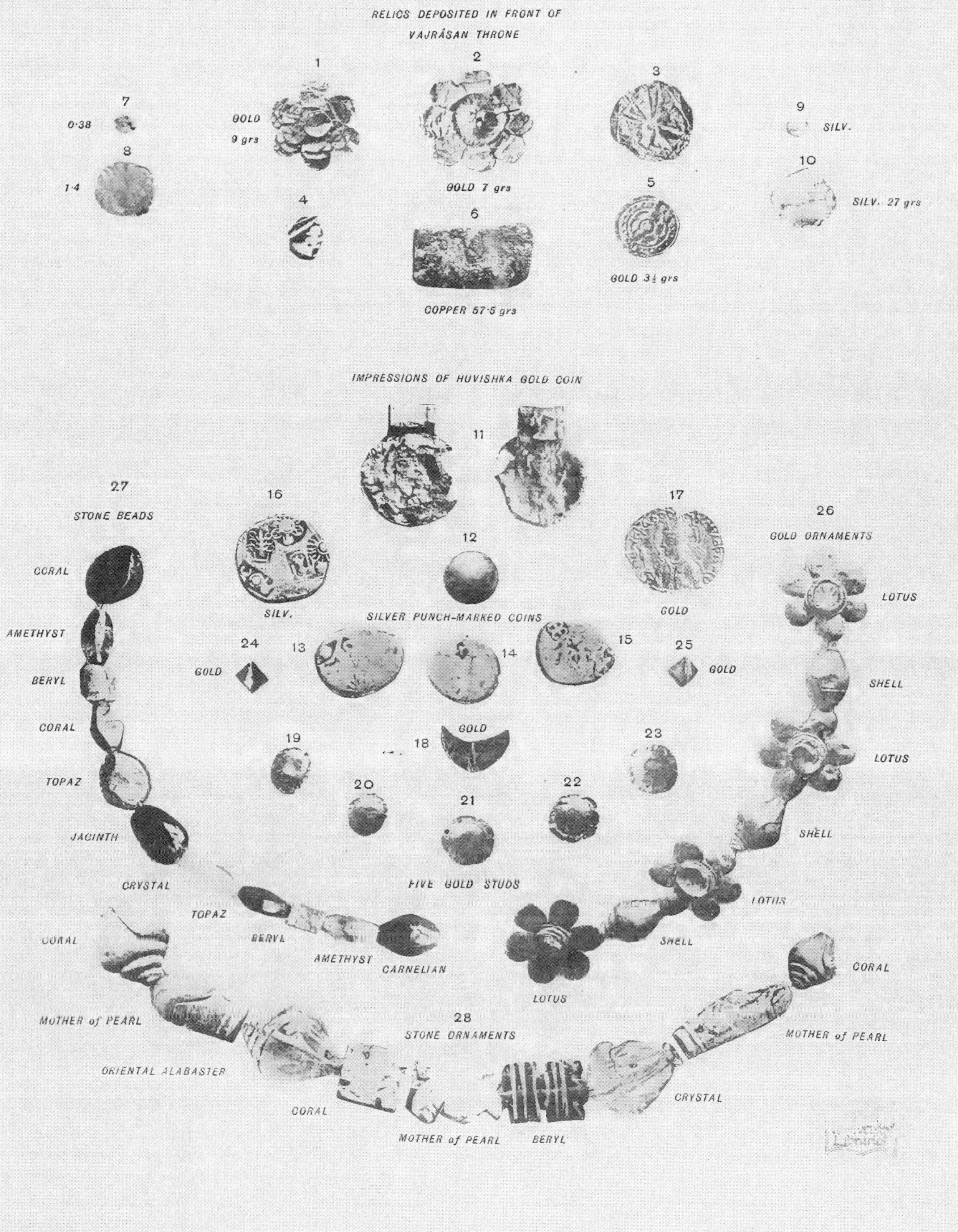
RELICS DEPOSITED IN FRONT OF
VAJRÂSAN THRONE
1
GOLD
9 grs
2
GOLD 7 grs
3
7
0·38
8
1·4
4
5
GOLD 3½ grs
6
COPPER 57·5 grs
9
SILV.
10
SILV. 27 grs
IMPRESSIONS OF HUVISHKA GOLD COIN
11
16
SILV.
12
17
GOLD
SILVER PUNCH-MARKED COINS
13
14
15
24
GOLD
25
GOLD
18
GOLD
19
20
21
22
23
FIVE GOLD STUDS
27
STONE BEADS
CORAL
AMETHYST
BERYL
CORAL
TOPAZ
JACINTH
CRYSTAL
TOPAZ
BERYL
AMETHYST
CARNELIAN
26
GOLD ORNAMENTS
LOTUS
SHELL
LOTUS
SHELL
LOTUS
SHELL
LOTUS
28
STONE ORNAMENTS
CORAL
MOTHER of PEARL
ORIENTAL ALABASTER
CORAL
MOTHER of PEARL
BERYL
CRYSTAL
MOTHER of PEARL
CORAL

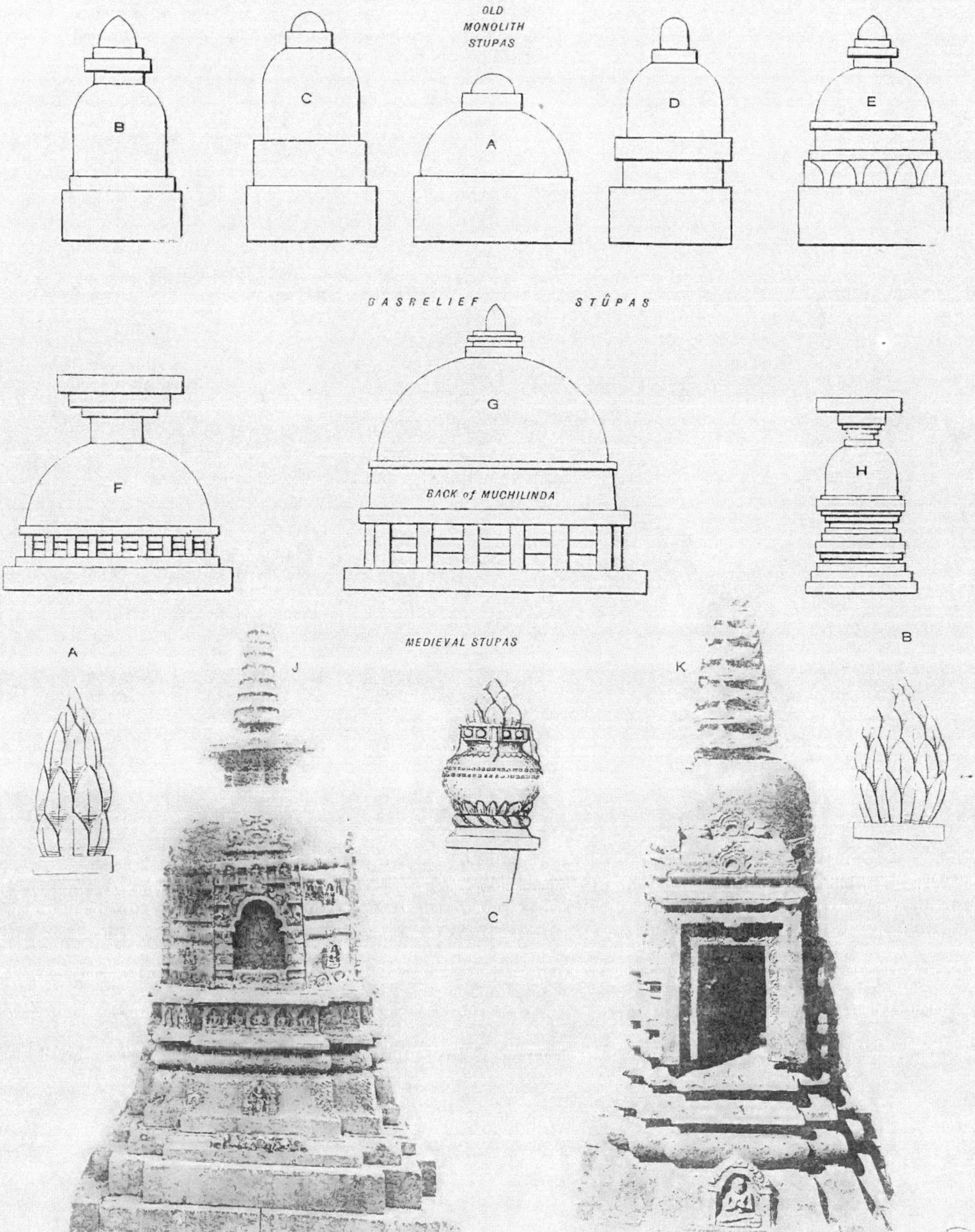

A. Cunningham, del.

MAHÂ-BODHI.

COLOSSAL STATUE of BUDDHA

INSCRIPTION on BASE of STATUE, dated S 64 = A.D. 142

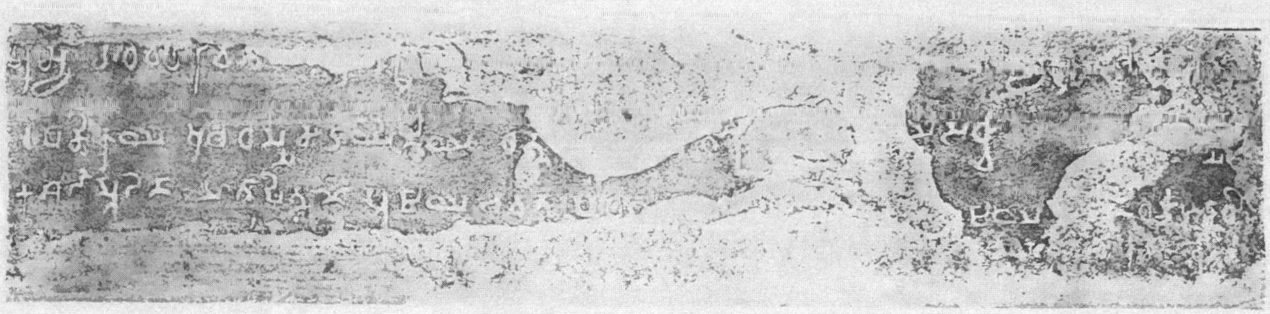

MAHÂ-BODHI.

TRIRATNA or BUDDHIST TRIAD

SANGHA BUDDHA DHARMA

SAKYA-MUNI
UNDER THE BODHI TREE

BUDDHA
TEACHING

1 — *INNER SIDE OF COPING OF S. RAILING*

C – *SATTAPANNI CAVE, RAJGIR*

COIN OF PASUPATI

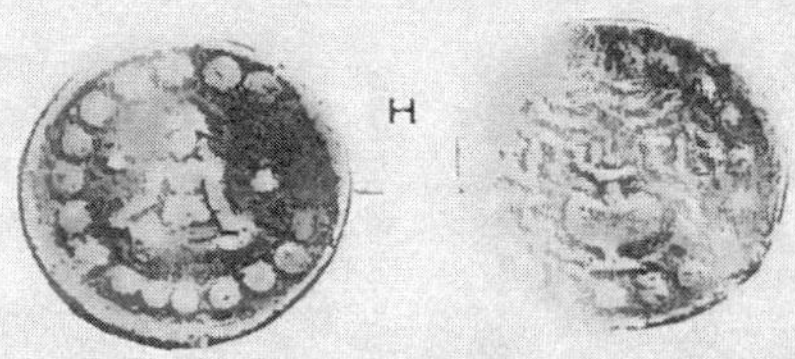

D – *NIRVÂNA STATUE at KUSINAGARA*

ROHTAS
G – *SEAL of ṢAṢANGKA*

E – *BACK OF MUCHILINDA STATUE*

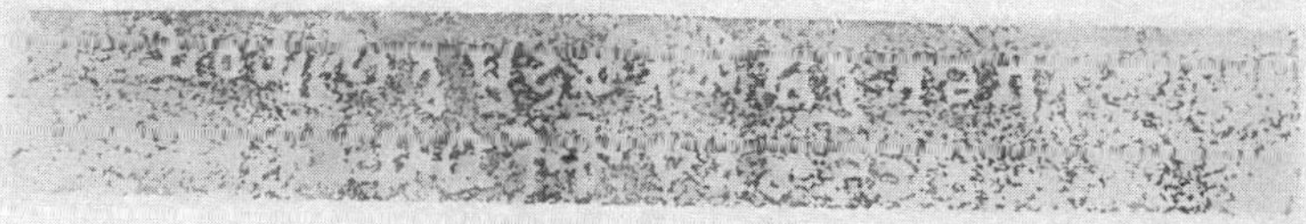

F – *FROM SMALL STÛPA*
Copper Plate

K – *FROM SMALL STUPA, Copper Plate*

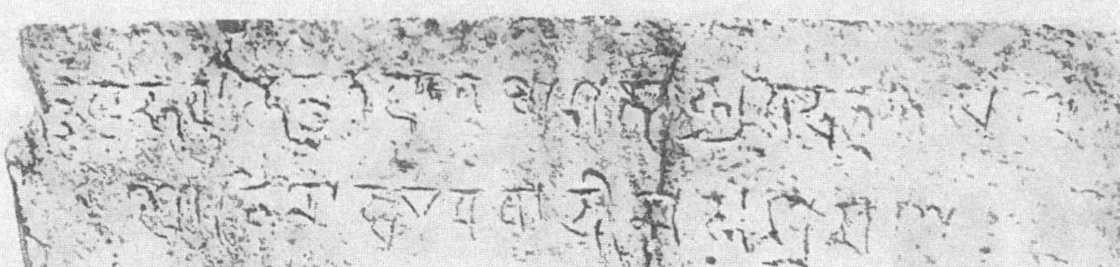

W. Griggs & Sons, Ld., Collotypers.

PEDESTAL OF STATUE

2-GOPÂLA, A.D-813-831

3-DHARMA-PÂLA, A.D. 850

F. BACK OF SMALL FIGURE

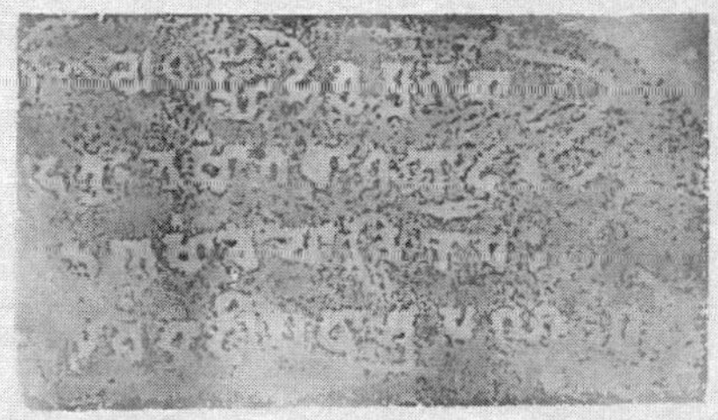

C
ASOKA-BALLA, Pavement

A
ASOKA-BALLA
A.D. 1157

INSCRIPTIONS on UMBRELLA

BURMESE

NÂGARI
hand copy

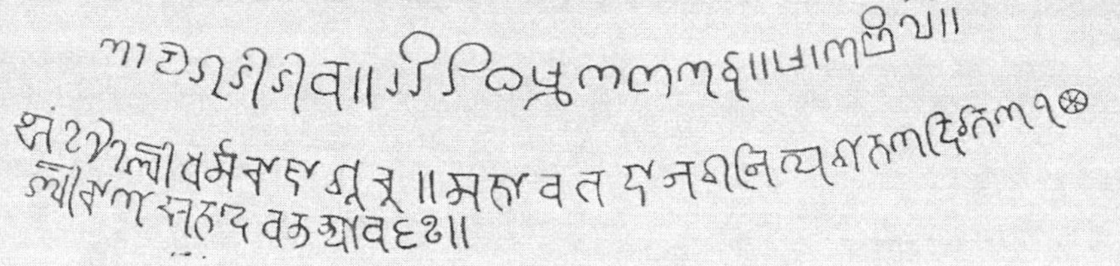

BURMESE

NÂGARI
photograph

INSCRIBED BRICKS of PINNACLE.

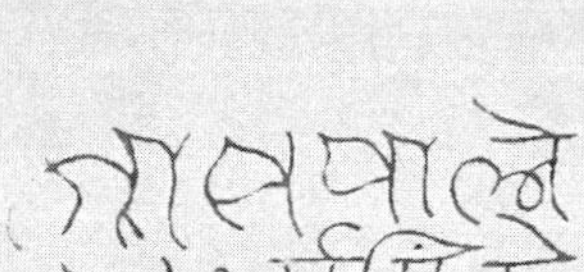

1. BENGALI

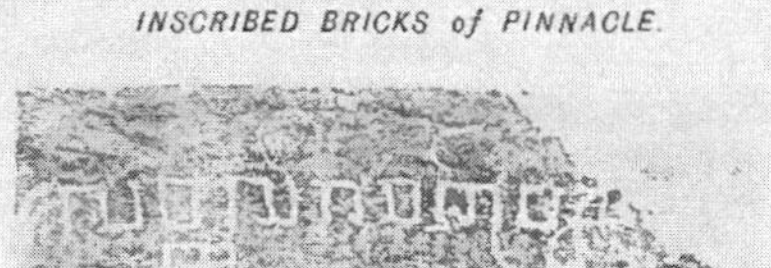

3 BURMESE

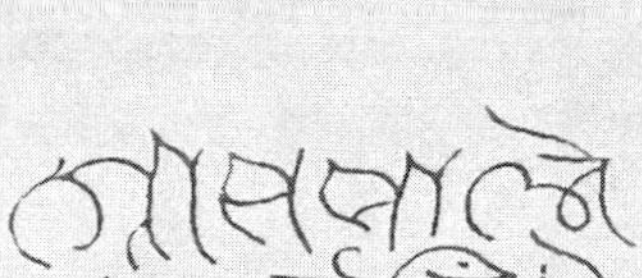

2. BENGALI

MAHÂ-BODHI.

1

VAJRA VARÂHI

2

3

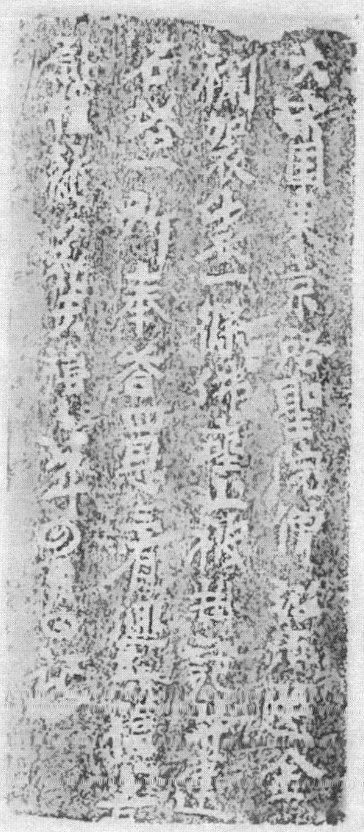

6